Statistics

and

Quality

Control

for the

Workplace

Also available from Quality Press

Quality Engineering Statistics
Robert A. Dovich

Final Acceptance Testing
Michael J. Muolo

Statistical Methods in Engineering and Manufacturing
John E. Brown

Concepts for R&R Studies
Larry B. Barrentine

Volume 1: How to Analyze Data with Simple Plots
Wayne Nelson

Volume 3: How to Test Normality and Other Distributional Assumptions, Revised Edition
Samuel S. Shapiro

Volume 9: How to Use Regression Analysis in Quality Control, Revised Edition
Douglas C. Crocker

Volume 10: How to Plan an Accelerated Life Test
William Q. Meeker and Gerald J. Hahn

Volume 11: How to Perform Statistical Tolerance Analysis
Neil D. Cox

Volume 13: How to Use Sequential Statistical Methods
Thomas P. McWilliams

Volume 14: How to Construct Fractional Factorial Experiments
Richard F. Gunst and Robert L. Mason

To request a complimentary catalog of publications, call 800-248-1946.

Statistics

and

Quality

Control

for the

Workplace

Frank C. Kaminsky, Robert D. Davis,
and Richard J. Burke

ASQC Quality Press
Milwaukee, Wisconsin

Statistics and Quality Control for the Workplace
Frank C. Kaminsky, Robert D. Davis, and Richard J. Burke

Library of Congress Cataloging-in-Publication Data

Kaminsky, Frank C.
    Statistics and quality control for the workplace/Frank C.
Kaminsky, Robert D. Davis, and Richard J. Burke.
        p.   cm.
    Includes bibliographical references and index.
    ISBN 0-87389-205-4 (alk. paper)
    1. Quality control—Statistical methods.   I. Davis, Robert D.
II. Burke, Richard J.   III. Title.
TS156.K346   1993
658.5'62'015195—dc20   93-12053
                                                            CIP

10 9 8 7 6 5 4 3 2 1

ISBN 0-87389-205-4

Acquisitions Editor: Susan Westergard
Production Editor: Annette Wall
Marketing Administrator: Mark Olson
Set in Janson Text by Linda J. Shepherd.
Cover design by Barbara Adams.
Printed and bound by BookCrafters.

For a free copy of the ASQC Quality Press Publications Catalog, including ASQC membership information, call 800-248-1946.

Printed in the United States of America

 Printed on acid-free recycled paper

 ASQC
Quality Press
611 East Wisconsin Avenue
Milwaukee, Wisconsin 53202

CONTENTS

4. Construction and Use of Control Charts

5. Process Capability Analysis

6. Putting It All Together

Index

Preface

This book was written to introduce workers at every level to the Deming philosophy of management, group problem-solving techniques, statistics, and statistical process control. It also is intended for individuals who teach these subjects. The text is the result of several years of teaching these subjects to a wide range of individuals, including hourly workers, supervisors, engineers, and managers. The ultimate objective of the book is to provide all workers with an understanding of the concept of variability, a common language (statistics) for meaningful discussion of a system's variability, and an overview of several problem-solving tools that are useful for understanding and improving systems.

Chapter 1 provides an overview of the Deming philosophy of management and emphasizes the importance of statistics in the Deming approach. While we feel quite strongly about the Deming philosophy and encourage everyone to study it, the most important point is that quality must become an integral part of any management philosophy.

Chapter 2 provides an overview of several problem-solving techniques that frequently are used by teams of individuals for improving the quality of a process. These include brainstorming, Pareto analysis, process flow diagrams, perfect process analysis, and fishbone diagrams. It must be remembered that quality is improved by *people*, not by statistics.

Chapter 3 introduces the important concept of *"thinking like a statistician."* In this chapter the subjects of basic random experiments and repeated random experiments are presented. These topics are essential for developing an understanding of variability and statistical process control. Histograms and summary measures are then introduced. Again, the purpose is to develop an understanding of variability and to lay the groundwork for understanding statistical process control and process capability analysis.

Chapter 4 discusses the process of trial control charting and then introduces several types of commonly used control charts; namely, p charts, c charts, $\bar{X}$ and R charts, and $\bar{X}$ and S charts. The emphasis is on the construction and interpretation of these control charts, rather than on their development from statistical theory.

Chapter 5 introduces the subject of process capability analysis. The two most common measures of process capability (PCI or C_p, and C_{pk}), as well as one-sided process capability measures, and their relationships to nonconforming parts per million (NCPPM) are discussed. At the end of the chapter, an example is provided to illustrate the danger of using a process capability index based on a single experiment to qualify a process. Again, the emphasis of this chapter is on developing an understanding of the subject, not on the mechanics of calculation.

Chapter 6 is an attempt to show how it all fits together. The philosophy, the group problem-solving tools, and the statistics must combine in a synergistic fashion, but this requires some strategic thinking. We suggest some of these strategies.

This text is not intended to be an exhaustive treatment of Deming's management philosophy or a detailed examination of the subjects of statistics and statistical process control. The objective, rather, is to provide an introduction to the basic skills and concepts that are essential to elementary statistical quality assurance. As such, it should serve as a solid foundation for building the knowledge and skills necessary for continuous process improvement. Listed at the end of each chapter are some significant sources for additional information regarding the chapter's subject matter.

Acknowledgments

The authors sincerely thank Jim Benneyan and Sandeep Saboo for their assistance in preparing this book. Deep appreciation is expressed to them for a tireless effort in proofreading, developing graphics, and editing. Their comments, suggestions, and contributions were invaluable. Without this dedication and assistance, the text would be incomplete.

We also thank the many clients who provided us with the opportunity to work and learn. Many managers, supervisors, and workers provided us with insights, and showed us interesting and challenging problems. We hope we have been able to convey those insights here.

> Improve quality, you automatically improve productivity. You capture the market with lower price and higher quality. You stay in business, and you provide jobs. So simple.
>
> –W. E. Deming

Chapter 1
The Deming Approach to Modern Management

The Deming Philosophy of Modern Management

In 1950, at the invitation of the Japanese Union of Scientists and Engineers, Dr. W. Edwards Deming introduced his philosophy of modern management to Japanese industrialists. Since that time Deming has demonstrated repeatedly that his philosophy works and that all organizations, both large and small, can benefit from the approach. As a result Dr. Deming is referred to by many individuals as the father of the third wave of the Industrial Revolution. The first wave involved the use of factories and modern machinery (for example, Eli Whitney and the cotton gin); the second wave dealt with mass production (for example, Henry Ford and the assembly line); and the third wave is characterized by the use of statistical methods to improve quality (for example, W. Edwards Deming and statistical process control).

A series of four videotapes, produced by the Encyclopaedia Britannica Corporation, provide an excellent introduction to the Deming philosophy of management. The first videotape, *The Five Deadly Diseases of Management*,[1] gives Deming's viewpoint on the problems of traditional methods of management. He identifies these problems in the context of five deadly diseases. Recently two additional diseases of management were added. The seven diseases are as follows:

Management's Seven Deadly Diseases

1. Lack of constancy of purpose, symptomized by short-term thinking, to plan product and service that will have a market and keep the company in business and provide jobs.

2. Emphasis on short-term profits—short-term thinking (just the opposite from constancy of purpose to stay in business), fed by fear of unfriendly takeover, and by push from bankers and owners for quarterly dividends, sacrificing long-range improvement in quality, product, and service.

3. Personal review system, or evaluation of performance, merit rating, annual review, or annual appraisal, by whatever name, for people in management, the effects of which are devastating. Annual merit rating is destructive to long-term planning, nourishes short-term performance, annihilates teamwork, and demoralizes employees. Management by objective, on a go, no-go basis, without a method for accomplishment of the objective, is the same thing by another name. Management by fear would be still better.

4. Mobility of management—job hopping. Good management takes a long time and requires knowledge of a company's problems, its production process, sales, service, and so on. Annual ratings encourage managers to move from one company to another in search of higher wages rather than put down roots.

5. Use of visible figures only for management. Equally important are figures that are unknown and unknowable; for example, the multiplying effect of a happy customer, or an unhappy one. Companies that don't take into consideration those figures will not survive.

6. Excessive medical costs.

7. Excessive costs of liability, fueled by lawyers who work on contingency fees.

The second and third videotapes, *Roadmap for Change, The Deming Approach*,[2] and *Roadmap for Change, Part II, The Deming Legacy*,[3] provide a case history on the implementation of the Deming philosophy of management at the Pontiac Fiero plant in Pontiac, Michigan. The fourth videotape, *Commitment to Quality, Roadmap for Change, Part III*,[4] examines the use of the Deming philosophy of management at

Zytec Corporation. These videotapes also provide a detailed discussion of Deming's 14 points for management.

Deming's 14 Points

1. Create constancy of purpose toward improvement of product and service, with the aim to become competitive and to stay in business, and to provide jobs.

2. Adopt the new philosophy. We are in a new economic age. We can no longer live with commonly accepted levels of delays, mistakes, defective materials, and workmanship. Western management must awaken to the challenge, must learn their responsibilities, and take on leadership for change.

3. Cease dependence on inspection to achieve quality. Eliminate the need for inspection on a mass basis by building quality into the product in the first place.

4. End the practice of awarding business on the basis of price tag. Instead, minimize total cost. Move toward a single supplier for any one item, on a long-term relationship of loyalty and trust.

5. Improve constantly and forever the system of production and service, to improve quality and productivity, and thus constantly to decrease costs and improve profit. It is management's job to continually work on the system.

6. Institute training on the job.

7. Institute leadership (see point 12). The aim of leadership should be to help people, machines, and gadgets to do a better job. Leadership of management is in need of overhaul, as well as leadership of production workers.

8. Drive out fear, so that everyone may work effectively for the company.

9. Break down barriers between departments. People in research, design, sales, and production must work as a team, to foresee problems that may be encountered in production and in use of the product or service. Optimize the company as a system.

10. Eliminate slogans, exhortations, and targets for the workforce asking for zero defects and new levels of productivity without providing methods.

11a. Use statistical methods for continuing improvement of quality and productivity, and eliminate work standards (quotas) on the factory floor. Substitute leadership.

b. Eliminate management by objective. Eliminate management by numbers, numerical goals. Substitute leadership.

12a. Remove barriers that rob the hourly workers of their right to pride of workmanship. The responsibility of supervisors must be changed from sheer numbers to quality. Improvement of quality will automatically improve productivity.

b. Remove barriers that rob people in management and engineering of their right to pride of workmanship. This means, inter alia, abolishment of the annual merit rating and of management by objective, management by the numbers.

13. Institute a vigorous program of education and self-improvement.

14. Put everybody in the company to work to accomplish the transformation. The transformation is everybody's job.

Three recent books, *The Deming Guide to Quality and Competitive Position* by Gitlow and Gitlow,[5] *Out of the Crisis* by Dr. Deming,[6] and *The Deming Management Method* by Mary Walton,[7] also provide an excellent discussion of the Deming philosophy of management.

In the videotapes and books it is stated repeatedly that quality is the responsibility of everyone in the organization and that quality must be led by management. This viewpoint also is expressed by many others. For example, Great Britain currently is involved in a national campaign to improve quality. As part of this campaign former Prime Minister Margaret Thatcher made the following statement:

> Responsibility for achieving competitive quality rests
> squarely with top management. But everyone in indus-
> try must recognize that quality is their business too.

As one examines the message that Dr. Deming brings to industry both the problem and the solution begin to emerge. Because of competition, the economic situation has changed and the traditional way of conducting business is not appropriate. The bottom line in the message is crystal clear: *Failure to change means failure to survive.* Accepting the fact that change is necessary, the alternative to the present way of conducting business is the Deming philosophy of management. This philosophy begins with the basic assumption that a company-wide attitude toward quality must be developed and that this development must be led by management from the top down.

The Deming approach is not simply a new program for an organization to implement. Deming adamantly asserts "There is no quick fix to resurrect American industry." The operational philosophy throughout the organization must radically change toward focusing on continuous improvement in quality, production, and service.

The Deming quality cycle is a process of continuous improvement in which equal balance is maintained in all four activities: plan, do, check, and act (PDCA cycle). The cycle involves all functions of an organization, including design, production, sales, customer service, and market research, and then redesign, in improving the quality of a process. New cycles begin based on experience gained from the previous cycle. In this continuous process of design and redesign, the level of quality is raised through prevention of recurring nonconformities.

In the Deming approach managers must take the position that an improvement in quality will lead to an increase in productivity and to a decrease in costs. Poor quality is driven out of the system and scrap and rework, which typically can account for as much as 20 to 25 percent of total operating costs, are reduced. This position is directly opposite to traditional thinking in which managers assumed that higher quality could be achieved only by decreasing productivity and by increasing costs.

In a modern quality assurance program it is assumed that the customer is the ultimate judge of quality and that the hidden costs of poor quality, such as the cost of a dissatisfied customer, must be taken into account. Levels of quality are sought which do not merely satisfy national or company standards, but which continually meet and exceed the requirements and expectations of consumers. When a company manufactures a product of poor quality, one of the following two situations is encountered.

- The customers don't complain and they go elsewhere.

- The product comes back but the customers don't.

Managers who fail to take into account the hidden costs of poor quality are considered by Deming to have one of the seven major diseases of management.

The quality of the process, which includes product design, materials, and production systems, can be evaluated more clearly by management.

Furthermore, sources of improvement and obstacles to improvement both lie in top management. With leadership by management, the quality of the process can be controlled and improved. This can be achieved only if everyone in the organization understands the system, if everyone becomes an inspector, and if everyone down the line is treated as a customer. Management must lead the way to improve the system and to achieve the ultimate objective of producing a product of high quality at a competitive price.

Any organization—be it for profit, nonprofit, a manufacturer of a product, or a provider of a service—can be viewed as a complicated system that consists of a huge number of operating subsystems. Each subsystem operates with inherent variability and therefore contributes to the inherent randomness of the overall organization. The Deming approach to management recognizes this situation. Modern managers must recognize that 80 to 95 percent of all variability is a direct result of the system itself and of the interactions between subsystems. Most variability is not the result of poor performance on the part of the worker.

The modern approach is to assume that any adversarial relationship between management and the worker is harmful to the organization's overall purpose—namely, to continue to stay in business by providing a better product or service at a lower cost. The worker and manager must communicate effectively and the communication must take place in a cooperative environment that is free of fear and punishment.

Employees work closely with the process nearly everyday, and therefore they should be treated as process experts. Their knowledge and insight are essential for process improvement. The Deming approach recognizes that the workers are in an excellent position to understand a particular subsystem and to make suggestions for improvement. A two-way flow of communication is desired in which the quality philosophy is spread by management through the organization and valuable information is then channeled up to management. This method of communication can be visualized as a two-way quality pyramid as shown in Figure 1.1.

In a modern quality assurance program, the role of management must be changed to that of improving the system. Deming suggests that traditional management by objectives be changed to that of management by involvement (MBI). From the chief executive officer down to the production supervisor, MBI must become the way of doing business. This approach requires major changes in everyone's attitudes. For the transformation to be successful, Deming states that a "critical mass of people must

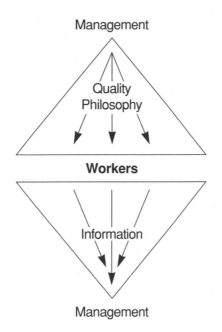

Figure 1.1   Two-Way Quality Pyramid

understand the reasons for a change and what the changes will involve."
Company-wide education regarding these changes and training in the
necessary skills are essential. Corporate executives must develop a corporate goal statement which emphasizes quality and deemphasizes
numerical goals related to growth and profit. The corporate goal statement should become a document that all people in the organization can
support with enthusiasm.

Those who practice MBI will be responsible for locating and eliminating all barriers to quality and productivity. One of these barriers is the
production quota. In the Deming approach production quotas are considered detrimental to the task of improving quality and productivity.
Similarly, the imposition of higher-quality standards (for example, zero
defects) without any change in the system is considered an unacceptable
practice. Artificial quality standards, production quotas, and performance
evaluation based on annual dividends and profit all create an environment
in which the worker and management are afraid to do the job. Fear is considered a major barrier to improved quality and productivity. In MBI, the
manager's job is to identify all situations which create fear and to change
the system to eliminate fear. Creativity, responsibility, risk taking, and

honest communication are all reduced by fear and, as a result, fear is considered to have a negative impact on quality.

In the past, managers who gained experience at several companies over a short period of time were considered to have upward mobility. This practice created managers who were unfamiliar with the system they were assigned to manage. It led to frequent process changes and managerial reorganizations. It also enhanced the practice of management by objectives with annual merit ratings and an emphasis on short-term profits. Mobility, annual merit ratings, and emphasis on short-term profits are considered by Deming to be three more of the seven major diseases of management.

Another major barrier to improved quality and productivity is found in the traditional practice of purchasing from suppliers who provide the lowest bid. In the Deming philosophy, modern managers must make a sincere effort to reduce the number of suppliers and to do business with only those who can demonstrate a dedication to quality. In this approach the purchasing department becomes directly involved and specifications to suppliers are written to emphasize quality.

Production quotas and fear are two factors that interfere with pride of workmanship. In the Deming philosophy, modern managers must identify all factors that have a negative effect on pride of workmanship. These factors must be eliminated and an environment must be created to enhance pride of workmanship.

The final two deadly diseases refer to Deming's concern that American industries are plagued by excessive costs of liability and medical care, robbing them of resources which would be better directed toward improving quality and productivity.

The Role of Statistics in the Deming Philosophy

In the practice of MBI it is assumed that 80 to 95 percent of all problems are with the system and not necessarily the worker. With this assumption, the role of management is to understand and change the system to make it operate with higher quality and productivity. In order to understand the system, numbers (the facts) will be collected from the system. These facts (numbers) will exhibit variability. In order to understand the system, managers and hourly workers will have to understand the subject of variability. Since statistics is the study of variability, it is absolutely essential to learn statistics to change the system. When management and the workers learn to communicate in the common language of statistics, then significant changes can be made to make the system operate with higher quality and productivity.

The Deming philosophy of management and the extent to which statistics is an important part of this style of management has been recognized by several companies. This recognition is clearly illustrated in a statement on quality that was published by the Pontiac Motor Division of the General Motors Corporation.

The Pontiac Quality Philosophy

Pontiac Motor Division commits itself to quality as our number one business objective. We are dedicated to operating under Dr. Deming's philosophy of management, including extensive application of statistical techniques and team-building efforts. We intend to be innovative and to allocate resources to fulfill the long-range needs of the customer and the company. We will institute better job training, including the help of statistical methods and will "do it right the first time," eliminating scrap and waste. We will provide a vigorous program for retraining people in new skills, to keep up with changes in materials, methods, design of products, and machinery, and in the use of statistical techniques to identify areas of improvement. We will reduce fear by encouraging open two-way communication. We renounce the old philosophy of accepting defective workmanship in everything we do—paperwork, processes, and hardware. We must eliminate the dependence on mass inspection for quality. We will maximize the use of statistical knowledge and talent in both our division and our suppliers. We will demand and expect suppliers to use statistical process control to ensure quality. Where possible, we will single source purchased items with the supplier who demonstrates the highest level of quality through statistical means.*

---

*This copyrighted statement is reprinted with the kind permission of the Pontiac Division of General Motors Corporation. Originally published a number of years ago, this statement has now been superceded, but the intent remains unchanged.

Chapter 2 discusses several problem-solving techniques useful in improving the quality of a process. Chapters 3 through 5 are devoted to the subject of statistics. The ultimate objective is to provide both management and hourly workers with a common language (statistics) that can be used to improve systems so that they operate with higher quality and productivity.

References

1. Encyclopaedia Britannica. *The Five Deadly Diseases of Management*, 1984.

2. ———. *Roadmap for Change, The Deming Approach*, 1984.

3. ———. *Roadmap for Change, Part II, The Deming Legacy*, 1986.

4. ———. *Commitment to Quality, Roadmap for Change, Part III*, 1989.

5. Gitlow, H. S. and Gitlow, S. J. *The Deming Guide to Quality and Competitive Position.* Englewood Cliffs, NJ: Prentice-Hall, 1987.

6. Deming, W. E. *Out of the Crisis.* Cambridge, MA: MIT Center for Advanced Engineering Study, 1986.

7. Walton, M. *The Deming Management Method.* New York: Dodd, Mead & Company, 1986.

Select Bibliography

Bowles, J. G. "The Race to Quality Improvement," *Fortune* (Sept. 1989).

Brooks, G. and Linklater, J. R. "Statistical Thinking and W. Edwards Deming's Teachings in the Administrative Environment," *National Productivity Review*, Vol. 5, No. 3: 271–80 (1986).

Conway, W. E. "A Change in the Management System," *Survey of Business*, Vol. 19, No. 3: 17–18 (1984).

———. "The Right Way to Manage," *Quality Progress* (Jan. 1982).

Deming, W. E. *Quality, Productivity, and Competitive Position.* Cambridge, MA: MIT Center for Advanced Engineering Study, 1982.

Drucker, P. F. *The Frontiers of Management.* New York: Truman Tally Books, 1986.

Gitlow, H. S. and Hertz, P. T. "Product Defects and Productivity," *Harvard Business Review*, Vol. 61, No. 5: 131–41, (Sept./Oct. 1983).

Halberstam, D. *The Reckoning* (Chap. 17). New York: William Morris and Company, 1986.

Hansen, L. "Rethinking American Management," *Managing,* 2, (1984): 3–4.

Lowe, T. A. and Mazzeo, J. M. "Crosby, Deming, Juran–Three Preachers, One Religion," *Quality,* Vol. 25, No. 9: 22–25 (Sept. 1986).

Main, J. "Under the Spell of the Quality Gurus," *Fortune,* Vol. 114, No. 4: 30–34 (Aug. 1986).

———. "The Curmudgeon Who Talks Tough on Quality," *Fortune* (June 1984): 118–22.

Mann, N. R. *The Keys to Excellence–The Story of the Deming Philosophy.* Los Angeles: Prestwick Books, 1988.

McMillan, C. J. "From Quality Control to Quality Management: Lessons from Japan," *Business Quarterly,* Vol. 47, No. 1: 31–40 (May 1982).

Mozer, C. "Total Quality Control: A Route to the Deming Prize," *Quality Progress,* Vol. 17, No. 9: 30–33 (Sept. 1984).

Nelson, C. A. "The Road to Quality Improvement," *Quality,* Vol. 23, No. 10: 51–54 (Oct. 1984).

Oakes, K. "Managing Productivity with Statistical Techniques," *CA Magazine,* Vol. 117, No. 2: 79–83 (Feb. 1984).

Port, O. "The Push for Quality," Special Report, *Business Week* (June 8, 1987).

Ranney, G. B. "Deming and the 14 Points: A Personal View," *Survey of Business,* Vol. 21, No. 3: 13–15 (1986).

Roth, J. "The Stuff That Quality Is Made Of," *Industrial Management,* Vol. 9, No. 7: 18–19 (Aug. 1985).

Scherkenbach, W. W. *The Deming Route to Quality and Productivity– Road Maps and Roadblocks.* Washington, DC: CEEPress Books, George Washington University, 1988.

———. *Deming's Road to Continual Improvement.* SPC Press, Inc., 1991.

Tribus, M. "Deming's Way," *New Management* (1983): 22–25.

Weaver, L. "Quality Control: Catalyst in Changing Industry," *Survey of Business,* Vol. 19, No. 3: 4–6 (1984).

Chapter 2
Problem Solving and Employee Involvement

Introduction

In the Deming philosophy of management, as a normal part of the new way of conducting business, an employee involvement group (EIG), or alternatively, a quality circle (QC), will be active in finding solutions to problems related to the quality of the process. Regardless of the name that is used, a group of people who have a good understanding of the process will jointly attack problems of quality. This situation was described appropriately by one employee as follows:

> I see. We, in the future, will be hired from the neck up instead of from the neck down as we were in the past.

These groups will evolve over time and, eventually, will operate with a formal structure. At the present time the type of structure that should be used is not well defined. There is, however, some excellent material on the success of certain structures that have worked in specific industries. For example, the Sperry Corporation has published a series of manuals for their quality circles training program.[1] In addition, Sperry has developed a videotape[2] on the subject.

Roger Milliken, the CEO of Milliken & Company and the recipient of the 1989 Malcolm Baldrige National Quality Award, offers the following testimonial to the payoffs due to employee involvement.

We have learned in our last nine years of concentrated effort on the quality improvement process that 80 percent of the breakthroughs have come from people who are actually working with the machines and computers on the plant floor or in the office . . . . Quality improvement comes from people on the job, not some genius in management.[3]

Regardless of the name given to the group, the people in the group will have to learn, in addition to statistics, a variety of problem-solving techniques and communication skills. Several of these techniques are discussed in this chapter. These include process flow diagrams, brainstorming, perfect process analysis, cause and effect (or fishbone) diagrams, and Pareto analysis.

Process Flow Diagrams

A process flow diagram is a tool for understanding a system. A common and clear understanding of the system is the necessary starting point for any meaningful discussion and process improvement. A flow diagram provides this description of the system and specifies the interrelations between specific steps and subsystems. A process flow diagram is a schematic description of how a system functions. Geometric shapes represent work steps, actions, events, and decision points, while arrows represent the flow of material, the flow of information, or the sequence of events. A sample flow diagram for the process of starting an automobile is shown in Figure 2.1.

In many situations, laying out the work flow as a flow diagram can be quite revealing. Differences in process understanding and work methods are highlighted and inefficiencies in the system are exposed. Every employee involved in the system must understand its process flow and should agree that the diagram is accurate. Disagreements should be addressed, resolved whenever necessary, and the process flow diagram revised.

As an exercise, try inviting a few friends to discuss the flow diagram shown in Figure 2.1. It is inevitable that such a discussion will lead to disagreement, resolution, and revision. Process flow diagrams should become an integral part of all future discussions and improvement efforts.

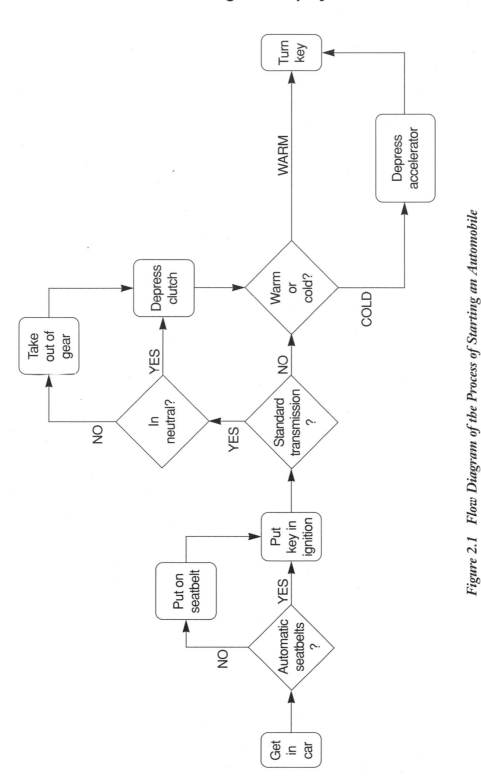

Figure 2.1   Flow Diagram of the Process of Starting an Automobile

Brainstorming

In general, brainstorming is a technique for generating a large number of ideas from a group of people who are familiar with a specific topic under consideration. A variety of rules and procedures have been developed to get the group to generate alternative ideas. All of them have the same general purpose, namely

- To generate ideas
- To stimulate creativity
- To learn and practice divergent thinking

Brainstorming usually works well with a small group of six to 12 people who have different backgrounds and a variety of experience with the problem. The brainstorming session also should be conducted by a group leader who has the following responsibilities:

- Brief participants on the problem and its background.

- Record all ideas on a blackboard or on a series of flip charts so that every idea is clearly visible.

- Provide each participant with a complete list of ideas that were generated during the session, arranged into related groups or ordered according to some priority system.

During the brainstorming session the group leader will have each person speak in turn while operating with the following rules:

- Criticism of an idea—*any* idea—must be withheld until the session is over. Nothing kills creative thinking more than the person who says, "Oh, that will never work."

- Freewheeling not only is permitted, but actually encouraged. The more unusual the idea the better. It is much easier to build on an idea than to come up with an idea in the first place.

- Quantity, as well as quality, is wanted. The greater the number of ideas, the greater the chances of getting some good ones.

- Hitchhiking is desirable. In addition to contributing ideas of one's own, each member of the group should think of ways in which suggestions of others can be built into better ideas, or how two or more ideas can be combined.

- Aim for 35 to 100 ideas.

- Allow people to say "pass."
- End the session when everyone passes.

Perfect Process Analysis

Perfect process analysis is simply a means to examine any process for inefficiencies. The purpose of perfect process analysis is to determine the amount of time, effort, material, and money that are wasted on quality problems. The results of a perfect process analysis should become the focus of statistical and other analyses which facilitate continuous process improvement. A final result of this analysis is an estimate of the cost of poor quality in the process.

Perfect process analysis basically means asking, via brainstorming sessions, what procedures and operations shown on the process flow diagram could be changed or eliminated if perfect (flawless, error-free) parts were received every time, and if all processes functioned perfectly. These procedures and operations should include all inspections and rework.

The procedures that are identified in this analysis have made poor quality acceptable. They exist only to compensate for system deficiencies or imperfect parts (for example, unpredictable system performance, parts which are beyond specifications, or incomplete or incorrect paperwork). They have resulted in promoting a system which accommodates poor quality. Such systems are costly and inefficient. The goal is to improve or to eliminate these inefficiencies.

The perfect process analysis should be applied to every step of the process as follows:

1. Understand the current system:

   a. Document the current system via process flow diagrams.

   b. Collect and analyze data from the system.

   c. Understand variability.

2. Label each procedure in the process as either Process, Transportation, Delay/Storage, Inventory, or Rework/Scrap.

   a. In the remaining steps, especially scrutinize procedures that are not labeled "Process."

3. Examine each procedure and ask the following questions:

   a. What is the cost of this procedure?

    b. Would this procedure be necessary if processes and parts were perfect?

      (i) If it is unnecessary, what is required in order to eliminate this procedure?

      (ii) If it is necessary, can this procedure be improved?

        (a) If the procedure can be improved, what is necessary to implement the improvement and what is the associated cost?

4. Estimate the overall cost of the current system and the overall cost of poor system quality. Remember that this estimate is, at best, a lower bound on the cost of poor system quality.

5. Prioritize the areas for improvement and elimination by using a combination of cost and ease of implementation.

Cause and Effect Diagrams

Cause and effect diagrams (sometimes referred to as Ishikawa diagrams) are graphical procedures for identifying those factors (causes) which may influence some quality characteristic (effect). They are also called fishbone charts because of the way they appear subsequent to construction.

On the fishbone chart the quality characteristic of interest is listed to the right of a bold arrow as shown in Figure 2.2. Stems to the main arrow are then constructed where each stem is characterized by a major grouping of factors such as people, materials, equipment, methods, money, and environmental conditions. Twigs (or fishbones) are then placed on each stem to identify in more detail those factors in each group which may have an effect on the quality characteristic. Twigs may then be placed on each twig until all factors have been identified. The actual construction of the fishbone chart encourages thought about the quality characteristic and, in this manner, it provides a useful exercise to identify problems.

Quality circles can effectively construct a fishbone chart using the chart as the basis for meaningful discussion. A clear understanding of the process leads to a detailed fishbone chart.

As an example on the construction of a fishbone chart, consider a spray painting operation in which the quality characteristic of interest is the number of bubbles in 100 square feet of painted surface. In a preliminary attempt to develop a fishbone chart, a group of people who are familiar with the operation identified the major factors as environmental

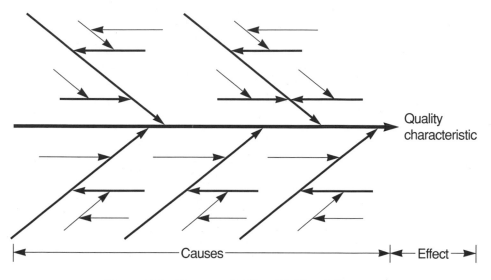

Figure 2.2   Cause and Effect (Fishbone) Diagram

conditions, equipment, surface characteristics, and workers. For each major factor important subfactors are identified and discussed. The procedure continues until the process is well understood and diagrammed as a fishbone chart. See Figure 2.3 for a preliminary attempt to construct a fishbone chart for this example.

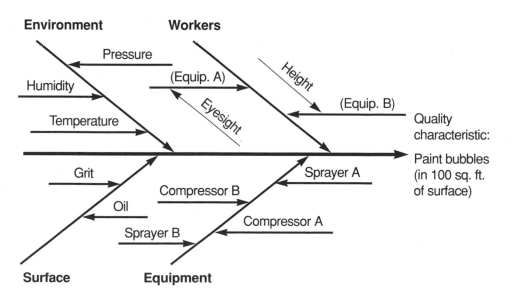

Figure 2.3   Fishbone Chart of Factors Affecting Number of Bubbles
in 100 Square Feet of Painted Surface

Pareto Analysis

The fishbone chart should be used in any initial examination of a process to determine significant factors that should be monitored through the use of a control chart. Other charts are also useful in this stage of analyzing a process. For example, the Pareto chart provides the analyst with a means of identifying those factors which may produce the most significant improvement in quality. In this manner, with limited funds and personnel, significant improvements may be realized quickly.

The Pareto chart is based on the Pareto Law which states, in essence, that if many factors are involved in an end result, a very few will be found to contribute a completely disproportionate share of the total. This law has been found to be true in many situations in quality assurance. A Pareto chart is simply a graphical procedure for ranking those factors which affect some quality characteristic so that the analyst can identify those which contribute most significantly to the end result.

As an example on the development of a Pareto chart, consider the consumption of electrical energy in a typical house. An analysis of monthly consumption of energy (in kilowatt hours) for the house might reveal the following factors as major contributors:

1. Hot water tank

2. Refrigerator

3. Clothes dryer

4. Washing machine

5. Small appliances

6. Lights

Suppose data on monthly energy consumption was collected for each factor. A typical breakdown of energy usage is as follows:

Factor	Percent of monthly energy
1. Hot water tank	45.0
2. Refrigerator	30.5
3. Clothes dryer	10.0
4. Washing machine	7.5
5. Small appliances	5.0
6. Lights	2.0

This situation, in graphical form, is shown in Figure 2.4 as a Pareto chart. A Pareto chart uses a bar graph, where the variable of interest is plotted in the vertical direction and the factors are listed in decreasing order of importance in the horizontal direction. In most situations the Pareto chart will clearly show the factors which contribute significantly to the total. In this case the hot water tank and the refrigerator are the factors to be considered as the best sources for major reductions in energy consumption.

The Pareto chart is also useful for comparing, in graphical form, before and after conditions. In this example it might decided to insulate the hot water tank. To determine the effect of this corrective measure, a second Pareto chart would be constructed.

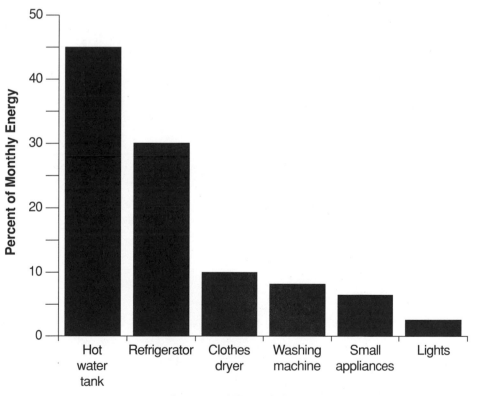

Figure 2.4   Pareto Chart of Monthly Electrical Energy Consumption

References

1. Sperry Corporation. *Quality Circles Training Program.* Computer Systems Education, P. O. Box 110, Princeton, NJ, 1983.

2. ———. *Quality Circles, The Sperry Approach.* Computer Systems Education, P. O. Box 110, Princeton, NJ, 1983.

3. Bowles, J. G. "The Race to Quality Improvement," *Fortune* (Sept. 1989).

Select Bibliography

Bemowski, K. "People: The Only Thing That Will Make Quality Work," *Quality Progress* (Sept. 1988).

Cornell, L. "Quality Circles in the Service Industries," *Quality Progress,* Vol. 17, No. 7: 22–24 (July 1984).

Hoerr, J. "The Payoff from Teamwork," *Business Week* (July 10, 1989).

Ishikawa, K. and Lu, D. *What Is Total Quality Control? The Japanese Way.* New Jersey: Prentice-Hall, 1985.

Juran, J. M. *Juran's Quality Control Handbook,* New York: McGraw-Hill, 1988.

Scholtes, P. R. *The Team Handbook,* Madison, WI: Joiner Associates, 1988.

Schoonmaker, A. L. "Creative Block-Busting," *ASQC Quality Congress Transactions,* Toronto, pp. 146–151 (1989).

Chapter 3
The Concept of Variability

Introduction: Thinking Like a Statistician

In the Deming philosophy of management it is assumed that 80 to 95 percent of all problems are with the system. The role of the modern manager, through MBI, is to understand the system and to change the system to make it operate with higher quality and, consequently, with higher productivity. The only way to understand the system is to understand the concept of variability and, since statistics is the study of variability, it is absolutely essential to learn statistics.

The primary topic of this chapter is the concept of variability. In order to understand variability one must learn to *think like a statistician*. This is not as difficult as it may sound. Each day everyone is exposed to situations that illustrate the concept of variability.

Random Experiments

The process of thinking like a statistician begins with the translation of a situation of interest into something called a basic random experiment.

1. Define an outcome of interest from a real world situation.

2. Does the outcome change?

3. Is the outcome unpredictable?

4. Is the experiment repeatable under essentially the same conditions?

If the answer is yes to each of the three questions, then the situation has been translated into a basic random experiment. Before delving more deeply into this concept, this four-step process is illustrated with several examples.

Example 3.1

Situation: A worker tests an ignition system.

1. Outcome of interest: Ignition system is good (performs properly; that is, conforming) or bad (does not perform properly; that is, nonconforming).
2. Obviously, the outcome may change from one ignition system to the next.
3. Although the outcome will be one of two possibilities, the result will not be known until the test is complete. It is, therefore, unpredictable.
4. For each ignition system produced or purchased, the experiment may be repeated under essentially the same conditions.

Example 3.2

Situation: An invoice is examined for errors.

1. Outcome: The number of errors found in the invoice.
2. The outcome may be any number from zero to the maximum number of entries that should have been made. It is presumed that omissions may be counted as errors.
3. The number of errors is unknown until the audit is completed.
4. The experiment can be repeated for each invoice under essentially the same conditions.

Example 3.3

Situation: A new work period begins.

1. Outcome: The number of people who are absent.
2. The outcome may be any number from zero to the total number of employees.
3. The number of people absent will not be known until the work period begins.
4. The experiment may be repeated each work period under essentially the same conditions.

In each of these examples, the number of possible outcomes is countable. Random experiments with a countable set of outcomes are called discrete. In these cases an integer value is normally assigned to the outcome of the experiment. This was an automatic result in Examples 3.2 and 3.3. This was not the case in Example 3.1. A statistician would assign either a 0 or a 1 to the outcome good and then either a 1 or a 0 to the outcome bad. The choice might be arbitrary. If the number of good or conforming items is of primary interest, then a 1 usually would be assigned to the outcome good.

Generally, a random experiment is classified as either discrete (if the outcome is countable) or continuous (if the outcome is measurable). This distinction is illustrated in Table 3.1.

Table 3.1   Classification of Random Experiments

	Type of outcome	
	Discrete	**Continuous**
Property	Countable	Measurable
Example values	0, 1 0, 1, 2, 3, . . .	1.1, 2.5, 9.4, ...0025, .0017, .0021, . . .
Physical correspondence of example values	Good, Bad Go, No Go No. of nonconformities, etc.	Length Area Volume Time

Random experiments for which the outcome is continuous are illustrated in Examples 3.4 through 3.6.

Example 3.4

Situation: A shipment of shoulder belts that are nominally 72 inches in length arrives and a shoulder belt is selected.

1. Outcome: The actual length of the belt.
2. The actual length may be any number greater than 0 but it will probably fall somewhere in the vicinity of 72 inches (for example, 73.6, 70.4, 71.9, . . .).
3. The actual length is unknown until the measurement is taken.
4. The experiment may be repeated for each belt in the shipment of belts and every time a shipment is received under essentially the same conditions.

Example 3.5

Situation: An employee who lives about 25 miles from work drives to work each day.

1. Outcome: The actual miles driven.

2. The actual number of miles driven will vary but will probably remain in the vicinity of 25 miles (for example, 25.2, 26.2, 24.9, . . .).

3. Until the employee arrives at work the miles driven will not be known.

4. The experiment may be repeated each working day under essentially the same conditions.

Example 3.6

Situation: An item is selected for a quality audit. A perfect item has a quality index of 100 percent.

1. Outcome: Actual quality index.

2. Any number that is no larger than 100 percent is a possible value (for example, 90.2, 85.7, 98.6, . . .).

3. Until the audit is completed the quality index is unknown.

4. The experiment may be repeated each time an item is available for an audit under essentially the same conditions.

Based upon the concepts illustrated in the previous six examples, a variety of situations that are encountered every day can be transformed into random experiments. Each experiment should be classified as to whether its outcome is discrete or continuous.

Repeated Random Experiments

The two characteristics of a random experiment that are extremely important to a statistician, and to the eventual concepts of statistical quality control, are that the outcome changes and is therefore *unpredictable*, and that the experiment is *repeatable* under essentially the same conditions.

If either of these characteristics is absent, then the random experiment is of no value. Generally, results from several repetitions of the basic random experiment, rather than the outcome of a single random experiment, form the basis for decisions. This repetition is viewed as follows:

Repeated random experiment

1. Define basic random experiment, called E.
   This outcome becomes *variable 1*.

2. Repeat basic random experiment a fixed number of times, say k.
   Call these k experiments $E_1, E_2, \ldots, E_k$.
   A variable 1 outcome is produced by each $E_1, E_2, \ldots, E_k$.

3. An overall outcome is computed from the individual outcomes. This outcome becomes *variable 2*.

   In statistical process control, variable 2 usually is monitored. Examples of variable 2 are the total number of nonconforming items, the average number of nonconforming items, fraction nonconforming, percent nonconforming, the average quality index of the k items, the average length of k shoulder belts, the average number of people absent in k days, the average number of miles driven to work in k days, and the average number of nonconformities in k invoices. This type of repeated random experiment is illustrated in Example 3.7.

Example 3.7

Basic random experiment: A worker tests an ignition system.

Outcome: The ignition system works (variable 1 = 0) or does not work (variable 1 = 1).

Repeat experiment 40 times

Experiment repetition: $E_1, E_2, E_3, \ldots, E_{40}$.

Individual outcome: 0 1 0 ..., 1.

Possible values for variable 2

1. Total number of nonworking items = outcome of E_1 + outcome of E_2 + outcome of E_3 + ... + outcome of E_{40}.

2. Fraction of nonworking items = total number of nonworking items divided by 40.

Additional second variables are introduced in later sections.

The Language of Statistics

The collection of measurements obtained from repetitions of the basic random experiment is a set of numbers. This set of numbers is referred to as the *data* from the composite random experiment. A *histogram* is a useful graphical display of the data. When the histogram is examined, important characteristics of the data and, by implication, the system from which the data were obtained become apparent. Both the *central tendency* of the data and the *variation* inherent in the data become apparent.

In this section the concept of the histogram is covered and calculations which are performed on the data set to summarize characteristics of the data are introduced. These calculations are called *summary measures*. They describe the central tendency and the variation of the data. The meaning of each summary measure is then illustrated through the use of a histogram.

In order to understand statistically the behavior of an operating system, an exact definition of the operating system of interest is required. Also the system has to be viewed as a random experiment. Once the random experiment is defined, the techniques to analyze the situation follow quite naturally.

Histograms for Discrete Random Experiments

The concept of a histogram is most easily understood in the context of a discrete random experiment. In this case the possible outcomes are countable and the histogram is easy to construct. The histogram is a direct graphical display of the data. The basic concepts are illustrated in Example 3.8.

Example 3.8

Basic random experiment: An invoice is examined for errors.

Outcome: The number of errors in the invoice.

Repeat the experiment 12 times with following results:

Experiment repetition: E_1 E_2 E_3 E_4 E_5 E_6 E_7 E_8 E_9 E_{10} E_{11} E_{12}

Outcome: 3   2   0   1   2   1   3   4   2   3   1   2

In this example, the outcomes consisted of the values 0, 1, 2, 3, and 4. A histogram of data from a discrete random experiment is a plot of the frequency of occurrence of each of the possible outcomes of the experiment versus the experiment's outcome. The frequency is simply the number of times that the outcome occurred. For this example we have the following:

Outcome	Frequency of occurrence
Numerical value	Number of times the outcome occurred
0	1
1	3
2	4
3	3
4	1
	Total 12

The histogram for this example is displayed in Figure 3.1. It shows very clearly how the outcomes are distributed with a central tendency of 2 and a range of values from a low of 0 to a maximum of 4. Again, a histogram of data from a discrete random experiment is a plot of the frequency of occurrence of the outcome versus the value of the outcome.

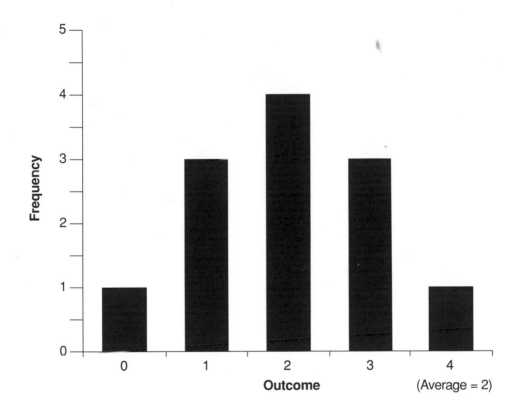

Figure 3.1   Histogram for Example 3.8

Summary Measures of Central Tendency

Prior to presenting histograms for continuous random experiments, it is desirable to have an introduction to the concept of summary measures. These measures convey information about the operating system from which the data were obtained. Summary measures of primary interest are related to the central tendency and the variation, or dispersion, of the data. Typical summary measures of the central tendency are

1. Average (or mean)
2. Mode
3. Median

The average (or mean) of the data is the sum of all of the individual outcomes divided by the total number of observations. In Example 3.8, the sum of the individual outcomes is 24, the total number of observations is 12, and the mean is $24 \div 12 = 2$. The same result is obtained if one multiplies the frequency with which a given outcome occurs times the value of the outcome and sums the results over all of the possible outcomes and then divides by the total number of observations. The average is denoted by $\bar{X}$ (pronounced *x-bar*). In our example

$$\bar{X} = \begin{array}{l} \text{sum of ((value of outcome) times (frequency of outcome)),} \\ \text{divided by the number of observations} \end{array}$$

$$\bar{X} = \frac{\text{sum of ((value of outcome)} \times \text{(frequency of outcome))}}{\text{the number of observations}}$$

$$\bar{X} = \frac{(0 \times 1) + (1 \times 3) + (2 \times 4) + (3 \times 3) + (4 \times 1)}{12} = \frac{24}{12} = 2.$$

The most commonly used measure of the central tendency is the average. It also is an important second variable in a composite random experiment. The average is the measure of central tendency that is used throughout this book. Although the mode and the median are not used they are defined briefly before further examples and discussion of the average.

The mode is the outcome that occurs with the highest frequency. It can be obtained visually from the histogram. The median is defined as the midpoint of the ordered data set, such that one-half of the outcomes are lower and one-half are higher. If the data set consists of an even number of observations, the median does not necessarily have to be one of the outcomes.

Example 3.9

Basic random experiment: A subassembly is inspected for faulty welds.

Outcome: The number of faulty welds.

Repeat the experiment 10 times with the following results:

Experiment repetition: E_1 E_2 E_3 E_4 E_5 E_6 E_7 E_8 E_9 E_{10}

Outcome: 2   1   3   2   1   0   1   2   1   2

In this example, the outcomes consisted of the values 0, 1, 2, and 3. The histogram for this example is given in Figure 3.2; it is based on the following summary of outcomes and frequencies of occurrence.

Outcome	Frequency of occurrence
Numerical value	Number of times the outcome occurred
0	1
1	4
2	4
3	1

Average of data for Example 3.9

$$\bar{X} = (0 \times 1 + 1 \times 4 + 2 \times 4 + 3 \times 1) \div 10 = 15 \div 10 = 1.5.$$

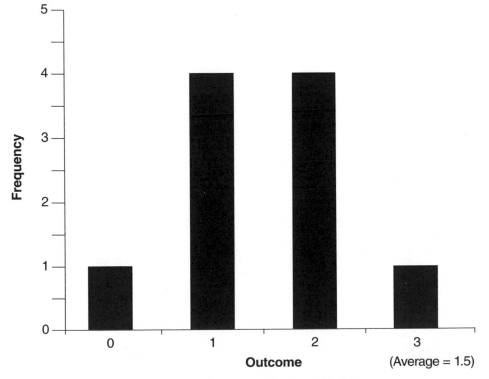

Figure 3.2   Histogram for Example 3.9

The average is always defined for a data set. It does not, however, have to be one of the possible outcomes of the experiment. In this example $\bar{X} = 1.5$ and it is not one of the possible outcomes (0, 1, 2, 3, 4, 5, . . .).

Example 3.10

Basic random experiment: A painted panel is inspected for nonconformities.

Outcome: The number of nonconformities.

Repeat the experiment 15 times with the following outcomes:

Experiment
repetition: E_1 E_2 E_3 E_4 E_5 E_6 E_7 E_8 E_9 E_{10} E_{11} E_{12} E_{13} E_{14} E_{15}

Outcome: 2   6   0   2   4   1   3   2   4   2   0   1   3   1   2

In this example, outcomes consisted of the values 0, 1, 2, 3, 4, 5, and 6. The summary of outcomes and their frequency of occurrence follow. The histogram for this example is provided in Figure 3.3.

Outcome	Frequency of occurrence
Numerical value	Number of times the outcome occurred
0	2
1	3
2	5
3	2
4	2
5	0
6	1

Average of data for Example 3.10

$$\bar{X} = (0 \times 2 + 1 \times 3 + 2 \times 5 + 3 \times 2 + 4 \times 2 + 5 \times 0 + 6 \times 1) \div 15 = 33 \div 15 = 2.2.$$

In this example the average is, once again, not one of the possible outcomes.

If the frequency of occurrence of each outcome is viewed as a weight placed on a bar at the position specified by the value of the outcome, the histogram gives a plot of the distribution of these weights along the bar. The average, $\bar{X}$, specifies where a support could be placed to balance the bar. This is illustrated in Figure 3.4.

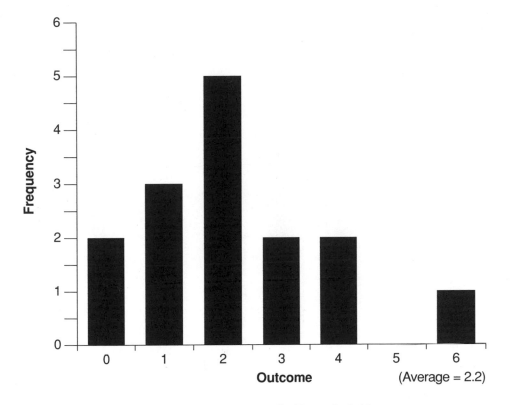

Figure 3.3   Histogram for Example 3.10

Histograms for Continuous Random Experiments

When the basic random experiment involves a discrete outcome, the histogram of the discrete data collected from repetitions of the basic random experiment is a straightforward plot of the outcomes versus the frequency of occurrence of each outcome. When the basic random experiment involves a continuous (or measurable) outcome, a histogram of the continuous data collected from repetitions of the basic random experiment is more involved. The fact that the number of possible outcomes can no longer be counted presents a complication.

A six-step procedure for constructing a histogram of continuous data follows. The procedure is simple. When the data set is large, however, it can require considerable effort. The procedure is illustrated with two examples. The primary difference between the histogram of discrete data and the histogram of continuous data is the definition of a cell. A cell for

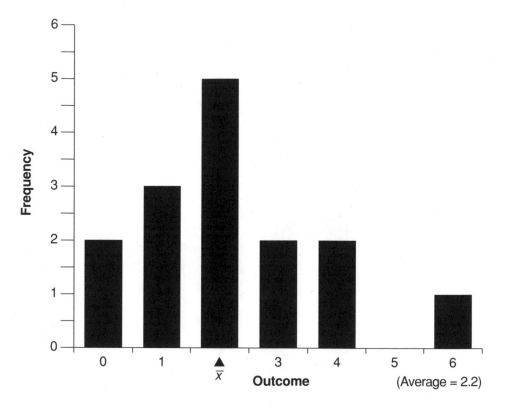

Figure 3.4   A Discrete Histogram Viewed as Unit Weights
Located at Value of Outcome

discrete data corresponds to the value of an outcome. A cell for continuous data corresponds to a lower boundary and an upper boundary. If an outcome has a value that is equal to or larger than the lower boundary of a given cell and is smaller than the upper boundary of the given cell, the outcome is said to be contained in that cell. Once the cells are defined, the histogram is easily constructed by simply counting the number of outcomes that fall within each cell. This frequency is then plotted versus the midpoint of the cell.

The six-step procedure is now presented and each step is illustrated for Example 3.11.

Example 3.11

Basic experiment: A subassembly is selected and the gap between two parts of the subassembly is measured.

Outcome: The distance between the two parts (to the nearest tenth of a millimeter) is the measurement.

Repeat the experiment 20 times with the following results:

Measurements in millimeters				
11.6	9.2	11.2	9.8	10.1
13.0	10.6	9.8	10.6	12.2
11.4	8.6	14.3	7.4	10.2
10.9	11.2	10.9	12.4	11.6

Six-Step Procedure for Constructing a Histogram of Continuous Data

Step 1 Order the outcomes from the smallest (minimum) value to the largest (maximum) value.

Step 1 applied to Example 3.11

Observation	Measure	Observation	Measure
1	(min.) 7.4	11	10.9
2	8.6	12	11.2
3	9.2	13	11.2
4	9.8	14	11.4
5	9.8	15	11.6
6	10.1	16	11.6
7	10.2	17	12.2
8	10.6	18	12.4
9	10.6	19	13.0
10	10.9	20	(max.) 14.3

Step 2 Choose the number of cells. Since no hard and fast rule exists for this step, the following guidelines are provided

Number of observations	Number of cells	Range for number of cells
Under 50	5 or 7	5 to 7
50 to 100	7 or 9	6 to 10
100 to 250	7, 9, or 11	7 to 12
Over 250	11, 13, 15, 17, or 19	10 to 20

For this procedure, an odd number of cells often is best.

Step 2 applied to Example 3.11

Since the number of outcomes (20) is under 50, 7 cells will be used. The choice of 7 is arbitrary.

Step 3 Determine the length of each cell (all cells will have equal lengths). The cell length is approximately equal to the largest value minus the smallest value, then divided by the number of cells. In order to simplify the remaining steps, the resulting value for the cell length should be increased to a reasonable value (0.476 increased to 0.5, 0.978 increased to 1.0, and so on). Note that the cell length should never be decreased.

Step 3 applied to Example 3.11

Largest value   = 14.3 (last value in ordered outcomes—see Step 1).

Smallest value   = 7.4 (first value in ordered outcomes—see Step 1).

Cell length (CL) = (largest value – smallest value) ÷ number of cells

$$CL = (14.3 - 7.4) \div 7 = 6.9 \div 7 = 0.986.$$

For ease of calculation this value is increased to 1.0.

Step 4 Determine the cell boundaries and the cell midpoint of the first cell as follows:

a. The *lower boundary (LB)* for the first cell is set equal to the smallest value observed or a convenient number that is smaller than this smallest value. For example, if 0.532 were the smallest value, $LB = 0.5$.

b. The *upper boundary (UB)* for the first cell is equal to the *lower boundary (LB)* of the first cell plus the *cell length (CL)*.

$$UB = LB + CL$$

c. The *cell midpoint (CMP)* of the first cell is equal to the lower boundary of the first cell plus one-half of the cell length *(CL)*.

$$CMP = LB + (CL \div 2)$$

Step 4 applied to Example 3.11

Cell 1:

a. LB = smallest observed value = 7.4.

b. $UB = LB + CL = 7.4 + 1.0 = 8.4.$

c. $CMP = LB + (CL \div 2) = 7.4 + (1.0 \div 2) = 7.9$

Step 5 Determine the cell boundaries and the cell midpoints of the remaining cells as follows:

a. The lower boundary of the second cell is the upper boundary of the first cell. The lower boundary of each subsequent cell is the upper boundary of the preceding cell.

b. The upper boundary of each cell is the lower boundary of the cell plus the cell length. Cells are added until the upper boundary of a cell is larger than the largest observed value.

c. The midpoint of each subsequent cell is equal to the midpoint of the preceding cell plus the cell length.

Step 5 applied to Example 3.11

Cell 2:

     a. $LB = UB$ of cell 1 = 8.4.

     b. $UB = LB + CL = 8.4 + 1.0 = 9.4$.

     c. $CMP = CMP$ of cell 1 + $CL = 7.9 + 1.0 = 8.9$.

Cell 3:

     a. $LB = UB$ of cell 2 = 9.4.

     b. $UB = LB + CL = 9.4 + 1.0 = 10.4$.

     c. $CMP = CMP$ of cell 2 + $CL = 8.9 + 1.0 = 9.9$.

Cell 4:

     a. $LB = UB$ of cell 3 = 10.4.

     b. $UB = LB + CL = 10.4 + 1.0 = 11.4$.

     c. $CMP = CMP$ of cell 3 + $CL = 9.9 + 1.0 = 10.9$

Cell 5:

     a. $LB = UB$ of cell 4 = 11.4.

     b. $UB = LB + CL = 11.4 + 1.0 = 12.4$.

     c. $CMP = CMP$ of cell 4 + $CL = 10.9 + 1.0 + 11.9$.

Cell 6:

     a. $LB = UB$ of cell 5 = 12.4.

     b. $UB = LB + CL = 12.4 + 1.0 + 13.4$.

     c. $CMP = CMP$ of cell 5 + $CL = 11.9 + 1.0 = 12.9$.

Cell 7:

   a. $LB = UB$ of cell 5 = 13.4.

   b. $UB = LB + CL$ = 13.4 + 1.0 = 14.4. Since this is larger than the largest observed value (14.3), it is the last cell.

   c. $CMP = CMP$ of cell 6 + CL = 12.9 + 1.0 = 13.9.

For clarity the above information is summarized in the following table:

Cell no.	LB	UB	CMP
1	7.4	8.4	7.9
2	8.4	9.4	8.9
3	9.4	10.4	9.9
4	10.4	11.4	10.9
5	11.4	12.4	11.9
6	12.4	13.4	12.9
7	13.4	14.4	13.9

Step 6 Record the number of outcomes (frequency) that is contained in each cell and plot the number of outcomes (frequency) versus the cell midpoints. In Step 1 all of the outcomes were ordered from smallest value to largest value of the observations. This greatly simplifies the counting procedure. Look down the list until the first observation that is equal to or larger than the UB of cell no. 1 (LB of cell no. 2) is found. Draw a line prior to this observation. Repeat this procedure for each cell. Find the next observation that is equal to or larger than the UB for the current cell (LB for the next cell) and draw a line prior to this observation. The number of observations for each cell is now contained between the lines drawn on the ordered observations.

The histogram for the continuous random experiments of Example 3.11 is shown in Figure 3.5.

One should note that the analogy of unit weights placed on a bar with a support located at the average value to balance the bar also applies to a histogram of continuous data.

Step 6 applied to Example 3.11

Number of observations	Cell number	Observation	Measurement	Comment
1	1	1	(min.) 7.4	
2	2	2	8.6	Larger than *UB* of cell 1
		3	9.2	
4	3	4	9.8	Larger than *UB* of cell 2
		5	9.8	
		6	10.1	
		7	10.2	
6	4	8	10.6	Larger than *UB* of cell 3
		9	10.6	
		10	10.9	
		11	10.9	
		12	11.2	
		13	11.2	
4	5	14	11.4	Larger than *UB* of cell 4
		15	11.6	
		16	11.6	
		17	12.2	
2	6	18	12.4	Larger than *UB* of cell 5
		19	13.0	
1	7	20	(max.) 14.3	Larger than *UB* of cell 6

Summary of the Six-Step Procedure for Constructing a Histogram of Continuous Data

Step 1 Order the outcomes from the smallest (minimum) value to the largest (maximum) value.

Step 2 Choose the number of cells.

Step 3 Determine the length of each cell (all cells will have equal lengths).

Step 4 Determine the cell boundaries and the cell midpoint of the first cell.

Step 5 Determine the cell boundaries and midpoints of the remaining cells.

Step 6 Record the number of outcomes (frequency) that is contained in each cell and plot the frequency versus the cell midpoints.

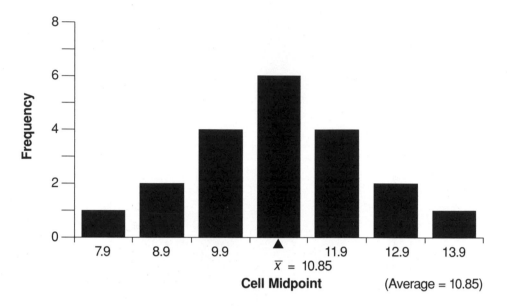

Figure 3.5   Histogram for Continuous Random Experiments of Example 3.4

Example 3.12

Basic random experiment: A sample is taken from a chemical process and the pH is measured.

Outcome: The actual pH measurement

Repeat experiment 24 times with the following results:

Samples	pH of Sample					
1–6	9.00	7.10	8.40	6.50	8.25	7.75
7–12	6.80	9.20	7.50	8.75	7.40	9.25
13–18	6.75	8.50	10.80	7.00	9.80	7.70
19–24	7.80	7.20	8.00	8.60	7.25	7.60

In this example certain cells will contain no observations.

Six-Step Procedure Applied to Example 3.12

Step 1 Order the outcomes.

Step 6 will be completed using the table of ordered outcomes.

Number of observations	Cell number	Observation	Measurement	Comment
5	1	1 2 3 4 5	(min.) 6.50 6.75 6.80 7.00 7.10	
8	2	6 7 8 9 10 11 12 13	7.20 7.25 7.40 7.50 7.60 7.70 7.75 7.80	Equal to *UB* of cell 1
4	3	14 15 16 17	8.00 8.25 8.40 8.50	Larger than *UB* of cell 2
6	4	18 19 20 21 22 23	8.60 8.75 8.90 9.00 9.20 9.25	Larger than *UB* of cell 3
1	7	24	(max.) 10.80	Larger than *UB* of cells 5 & 6*

*Cell 5 and cell 6 have zero (0) observations in the cell.

Step 2 Choose the number of cells.

Since the number of observations, 24, is less than 50, seven cells will be used. Again, five cells could be used if desired.

Step 3 Determine the *CL*.

Largest value = 10.80 (last value in ordered outcomes).

Smallest value = 6.50 (first value in ordered outcomes).

$CL = (10.80 - 6.50) \div 7 = 0.614$. This value is increased to 0.70.

Step 4 Determine *LB*, *UB*, and *CMP* for cell 1.

$LB = 6.50.$

$UB = LB + CL = 6.50 + 0.70 = 7.20.$

$CMP = LB + CL \div 2 = 6.50 + 0.70 \div 2 = 6.85.$

Step 5 Determine *LB*, *UB*, and *CMP* for the remaining cells.

Cell no.	LB	UB	CMP	
1	6.50	7.20	6.85	(CL = 0.70)
2	7.20	7.90	7.55	
3	7.90	8.60	8.25	
4	8.60	9.30	8.95	
5	9.30	10.00	9.65	
6	10.00	10.70	10.35	
7	10.70	11.40*	11.05	

*Larger than the largest observed value.

Note that once the *LB*, *UB*, and *CMP* are determined for the first cell, the *LB*, *UB*, and *CMP* for each subsequent cell are obtained by simply adding the cell length to the previous corresponding values.

Step 6 Record the frequency for each cell and plot the frequency versus the *CMP*. The frequency was obtained in the ordered table for Step 1. The histogram of the continuous random experiments of Example 3.12 is shown in Figure 3.6.

The Bell-Shaped Histogram and Summary Measures

In many situations the histogram of continuous data has the form illustrated in Figure 3.7. This type of histogram will be referred to as a *bell-shaped histogram*. Due to the fact that bars are used to represent the frequency of occurrence, the histogram may not appear to be bell-shaped. If a smooth curve is used to represent the frequency of occurrence (as shown in Figure 3.8), the result definitely is bell-shaped. When this special shape occurs, there are very interesting and important characteristics of the underlying data. These will be covered later in this chapter. They are important for later chapters on control charts and process capability.

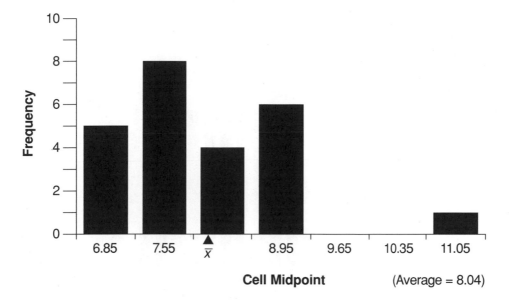

Figure 3.6   Histogram for Continuous Random Experiments of Example 3.12

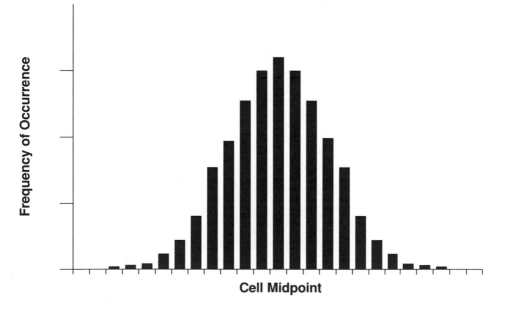

Figure 3.7   A Bell-Shaped Histogram

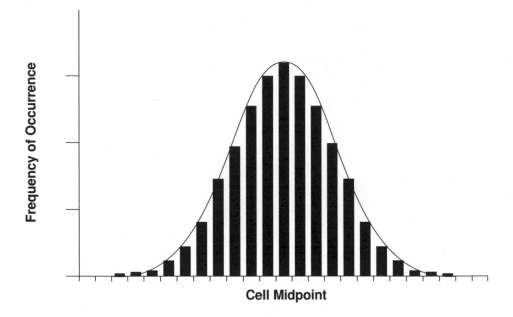

Figure 3.8   Bell-Shaped Histogram with Smooth Curve to Represent Frequency

Summary Measures of Variability

Summary measures of the central tendency of a data set were presented earlier. A second type of summary measure is used to describe the variability (dispersion or spread) in the data set. The most common measures are

1. Range (maximum – minimum)

2. Variance

3. Standard deviation

These terms are used in discussing variability of both discrete and continuous data sets. Each of these are defined and calculated for the data sets of the previous examples as shown on page 45.

The maximum is the largest number in the data set. The minimum is the smallest number in the data set. If a histogram was constructed using the six-step procedure, the minimum is always the first number in the ordered data set and the maximum is always the last number in the ordered data set. The range is the maximum minus the minimum, that is,

$$Range = Maximum - Minimum$$

Previous example	Type of basic experiment	Data set	Average $\bar{X}$
3.8	Discrete	3, 2, 0, 1, 2, 1, 3, 4, 2, 3, 1, 2	2.00
3.10	Discrete	2, 6, 0, 2, 4, 1, 3, 2, 4, 2, 0, 1, 3, 1, 2	2.20
3.11	Continuous	11.6, 9.2, 11.2, 9.8, 10.1, 13.0, 10.6, 9.8, 10.6, 12.2, 11.4, 8.6, 14.3, 7.4, 10.2, 10.9, 11.2, 10.9, 12.4, 11.6	10.85
3.12	Continuous	9.00, 7.10, 8.40, 6.50, 8.25, 7.75, 6.80, 9.20, 7.50, 8.75, 7.40, 9.25, 6.75, 8.50, 10.80, 7.00, 8.90, 7.70, 7.80, 7.20, 8.00, 8.60, 7.25, 7.60	8.04

These values for the selected examples are

Summary measure	Example			
	3.8	**3.10**	**3.11**	**3.12**
Maximum	4	6	14.3	10.80
Minimum	0	0	7.4	6.50
Range = Maximum – Minimum	4	6	6.9	4.30

These terms provide information about the underlying process with respect to the size of the largest and smallest outcomes expected and also about the spread in the values of the outcomes. Although they are simple to determine, they are important for applications in control charts. The range can be used to obtain estimates of the more complex measures of variability called the variance and the standard deviation of the data set. It also is an important second variable.

In order to obtain the variance of the data set, one first calculates for each observation the following term:

Value of the outcome minus the average, squared

The variance is the sum of all these resulting terms, divided by one less than the number of observations. The standard deviation of the data set is the positive square root of the variance. Prior to calculating these two summary measures for the examples, a smaller example will be used for illustration.

Example 3.13

Data set: 3, 4, 5, 6, 7

Number of observations = 5

Average $= \bar{X} = (3 + 4 + 5 + 6 + 7) \div 5 = 25 \div 5 = 5.0$

Observation number	Outcome or value*	Value squared*	$\bar{X}$	Value minus $\bar{X}$	(Value minus $\bar{X}$) squared
1	3	9	5	–2	4
2	4	16	5	–1	1
3	5	25	5	0	0
4	6	36	5	1	1
5	7	49	5	2	4
Sum of columns	25	135	25	0	10

$$\text{Variance of data set} = s^2 = \frac{\text{sum of all the ((value minus } \bar{X}) \text{ squared) terms}}{(\text{number of observations minus one})}$$

$$= \frac{10}{5-1} = \frac{10}{4} = 2.5.$$

Standard deviation of data set $= s =$ square root of variance

$= $ square root of 2.5 = 1.58.

The variance of the data set may also be calculated as follows:

$$s^2 = \frac{\text{sum of all (value squared) terms} - (\text{number of observations} \times (\bar{X} \text{ squared}))}{\text{the number of observations} - \text{one}}$$

This result for Example 3.13 is:

$$s^2 = \frac{(135 - (5 \times (5^2)))}{5-1} = \frac{(135 - (5 \times 25))}{4}$$

$$= \frac{135 - 125}{4} = \frac{10}{4} = 2.5.$$

---

*The second and third columns will be used later to illustrate a second, and easier, procedure to calculate the variance, and hence the standard deviation.

In both procedures the standard deviation is calculated as the square root of the variance.

The second procedure for calculating the variance and the standard deviation will be used for Examples 3.8 and 3.10 through 3.12. Calculation of $\bar{X}$, s^2, and s are summarized as follows:

1. Tabulate the data as shown in Tables 3.2 and 3.3.

2. Record the observation number in column 1.

3. Record the value of the observation in column 2.

4. Record the value of the observation squared in column 3. This is simply the square of the number recorded in column 2.

5. Add the numbers recorded in column 2 and divide this total by the number of observations (the last number recorded in column 1). The result is $\bar{X}$.

6. Add the numbers in column 3. This is the sum of all the (value squared) terms.

7. Calculate s^2 as follows:

$$s^2 = \frac{(\text{sum of column 3}) - (\text{number of observations}) \times \bar{X}^2}{(\text{number of observations} - 1)}$$

8. s = square root of s^2 (denoted by $\sqrt{s^2}$).

All of the calculations for these four examples are demonstrated as follows:

Example 3.8 *(Revisited)*

Number of observations = 12,

Sum of column 2 of Table 3.2 = 24,

$$\bar{X} = \frac{24}{12} = 2, \qquad\qquad \bar{X}^2 = 4,$$

Sum of column 3 of Table 3.2 = 62,

Number of observations − 1 = 12 − 1 = 11,

$$s^2 = \frac{62 - (12)(4)}{11} = \frac{(62 - 48)}{11} = \frac{14}{11} = 1.2727,$$

$$s = \sqrt{s^2} = \sqrt{1.2727} = 1.128.$$

Table 3.2

Example 3.8			Example 3.10		
No.	Outcome or value	Value squared	No.	Outcome or value	Value squared
1	3	9	1	2	4
2	2	4	2	6	36
3	0	0	3	0	0
4	1	1	4	2	4
5	2	4	5	4	16
6	1	1	6	1	1
7	3	9	7	3	9
8	4	16	8	2	4
9	2	4	9	4	16
10	3	9	10	2	4
11	1	1	11	0	0
12	2	4	12	1	1
			13	3	9
			14	1	1
			15	2	4
Sum of column	24	62	Sum of column	33	109

Example 3.10 *(Revisited)*

Number of observations = 15,

Sum of column 5 of Table 3.2 = 33,

$$\bar{X} = \frac{33}{15} = 2.2, \qquad \bar{X}^2 = 4.84,$$

Sum of column 6 of Table 3.2 = 109,

Number of observations − 1 = 15 − 1 = 14,

$$s^2 = \frac{109 - (15)(4.84)}{14} = \frac{(109 - 72.6)}{14} = \frac{36.4}{14} = 2.6,$$

$$s = \sqrt{s^2} = \sqrt{2.6} = 1.612.$$

Table 3.3

	Example 3.11			Example 3.12	
No.	**Outcome or value**	**Value squared**	**No.**	**Outcome or value**	**Value squared**
1	11.6	134.56	1	9.00	81.00
2	9.2	84.64	2	7.10	50.41
3	11.2	125.44	3	8.40	70.56
4	9.8	96.04	4	6.50	42.25
5	10.1	102.01	5	8.25	68.0625
6	13.0	169.00	6	7.75	60.0625
7	10.6	112.36	7	6.80	46.24
8	9.8	96.04	8	9.20	84.64
9	10.6	112.36	9	7.50	56.25
10	12.2	148.84	10	8.75	76.5625
11	11.4	129.96	11	7.40	54.76
12	8.6	73.96	12	9.25	85.5625
13	14.3	204.49	13	6.75	45.5625
14	7.4	54.76	14	8.50	72.25
15	10.2	104.04	15	10.80	116.64
16	10.9	118.81	16	7.00	49.00
17	11.2	125.44	17	8.90	79.21
18	10.9	118.81	18	7.70	59.29
19	12.4	153.76	19	7.80	60.84
20	11.6	134.56	20	7.20	51.84
			21	8.00	64.00
			22	8.60	73.96
			23	7.25	52.5625
			24	7.60	57.76
Sum of column	217.0	2399.88	Sum of column	192.0	1559.275

Example 3.11 *(Revisited)*

Number of observations = 20,

Sum of column 2 of Table 3.3 = 217.0,

$$\bar{X} = \frac{217.0}{20} = 10.85, \qquad \bar{X}^2 = 117.7225,$$

Sum of column 3 of Table 3.3 = 2399.88,

Number of observations − 1 = 20 − 1 = 19,

$$s^2 = \frac{2399.88 - (20)(117.7225)}{19} = \frac{(2399.88 - 2354.45)}{19}$$

$$= \frac{45.43}{19} = 2.391,$$

$$s = \sqrt{s^2} = \sqrt{2.391} = 1.546.$$

Example 3.12 *(Revisited)*

Number of observations = 24,

Sum of column 5 of Table 3.3 = 192.0,

$$\bar{X} = \frac{192.0}{24} = 8, \qquad \bar{X}^2 = 64,$$

Sum of column 6 of Table 3.3 = 1559.275,

Number of observations − 1 = 24 − 1 = 23,

$$s^2 = \frac{1559.275 - (24)(64)}{23} = \frac{(1559.275 - 1536)}{23}$$

$$= \frac{23.275}{23} = 1.0120,$$

$$s = \sqrt{s^2} = \sqrt{1.0120} = 1.006.$$

This section has emphasized the mechanics of calculating summary measures of variability. It should be reasonably clear that the average is a measure of the central tendency of a data set and that the range is a measure of the variability or spread in the data set. It is doubtful, however, that the variance and the standard deviation are as easily understood as measures of the variability of the data set. The following sections address understanding and interpreting these two summary measures.

The Importance of the Bell-Shaped Histogram

If a data set has the bell-shaped histogram, such as Figure 3.8, the average $\bar{X}$ and the standard deviation s provide important information about the data set, and hence about the process from which the data were taken. For data with a bell-shaped histogram, it is known that

- 68.27 percent of all observations are contained between $\bar{X} - s$ and $\bar{X} + s$

- 95.45 percent of all observations are contained between $\bar{X} - 2 \times s$ and $\bar{X} + 2 \times s$

- 99.73 percent of all observations are contained between $\bar{X} - 3 \times s$ and $\bar{X} + 3 \times s$

In fact the percent of observations contained in any interval can be determined in terms of $\bar{X}$ and s.

In the case of a bell-shaped histogram, the standard deviation describes the variability of the data in a more precise way than the range. The range simply tells the *distance* between the smallest and the largest observation, whereas the standard deviation and the average describe the *distribution* of the observations about the central tendency. Similar information can be obtained for a variety of histograms.

Many continuous random experiments, such as ones that have weight or a dimension (length, width, height) as a measurement, will result in data which have an approximately bell-shaped histogram. Another important aspect of this histogram, addressed in Subgroups, is that it applies to averages of groups of data.

Recall that the data for Example 3.11 resulted in an approximately bell-shaped histogram. If the above results are applied to this example, the following results are obtained:

1. $\bar{X} = 10.85$ and $s = 1.546$, see Table 3.3 and the calculation of s.

2. The distribution of observations about the central tendency is

    a. 68.27 percent from $\bar{X} - s$ to $\bar{X} + s$

    $\bar{X} - s = 10.85 - 1.546 = 9.304$

    $\bar{X} + s = 10.85 + 1.546 = 12.396$

    Actual number of observations in this interval was 14 out of 20 or 70 percent.

b. 95.44 percent from $\bar{X} - 2 \times s$ to $\bar{X} + 2 \times s$

$\bar{X} - 2 \times s = 10.85 - 2 \times (1.546) = 7.758$

$\bar{X} + 2 \times s = 10.85 + 2 \times (1.546) = 13.942$

Actual number of observations in this interval was 18 out of 20 or 90 percent.

c. 99.73 percent from $\bar{X} - 3 \times s$ to $\bar{X} + 3 \times s$

$\bar{X} - 3 \times s = 10.85 - 3 \times (1.546) = 6.212$

$\bar{X} + 3 \times s = 10.85 + 3 \times (1.546) = 15.488$

All, or 100 percent, of the observations were in this interval.

These intervals are illustrated in Figure 3.9. If more data were obtained from this process, the results would improve.

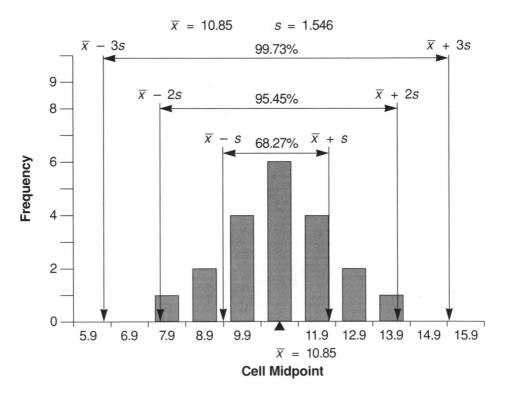

Figure 3.9   Histogram of Data for Example 3.11
Illustration of Standard Deviation as a Measure of Variability

A histogram of 5000 data points is given in Figure 3.10. $\bar{X}$ for this measurement is 100.00 and $s = 10.00$. Since the histogram is approximately bell-shaped, the percentage of observations contained in the three intervals can be predicted. These predictions and the actual results are:

Interval		Predicted		Actual	
From	**To**	**Number**	**Percent**	**Number**	**Percent**
$\bar{X} - s = 90$	$\bar{X} + s = 110$	3413	68.27	3378	67.56
$\bar{X} - 2 \times s = 80$	$\bar{X} + 2 \times s = 120$	4772	95.45	4773	95.46
$\bar{X} - 3 \times s = 70$	$\bar{X} + 3 \times s = 130$	4987	99.73	4889	97.78

These intervals are illustrated in Figure 3.10.

If it is known that a data set has a bell-shaped histogram and the average $\bar{X}$ and standard deviation s are known, then important information is readily available. For example, if a data set has a bell-shaped histogram with $\bar{X} = 100$ and $s = 10$, it is known immediately that the following is true:

Interval	Percent of observations contained in the interval
90 to 110	68.27
80 to 120	95.45
70 to 130	99.73

The random experiment may involve a product dimension subject to engineering specifications. For example, if the upper specification limit (USL) on this measurement is at or above 130 and if the lower specification limit (LSL) is at or below 70, very little nonconforming product is being produced. If, however, USL = 110 and LSL = 90, then 31.74 percent of all the product produced fails to meet the specifications. By using information provided in later chapters, this concept can be applied for any specifications and the fraction of acceptable (or nonconforming) product can be determined.

Subgroups

A subgroup is an extension of a repeated random experiment. If a basic random experiment is repeated k times, a set of k observations is

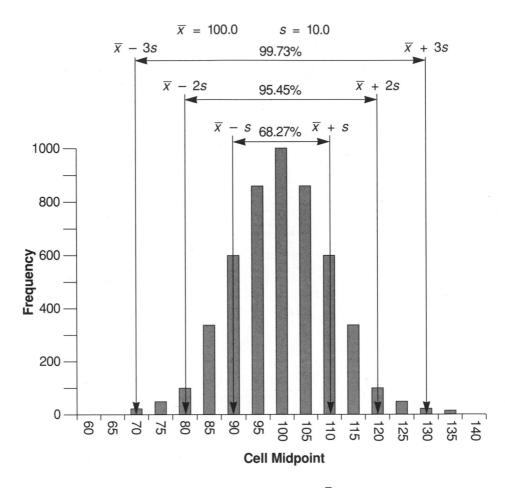

*Figure 3.10   Histogram of 5000 Data Points, $\bar{X}$ = 100.0 and s = 100,
to Illustrate the Standard Deviation as a Measure of Variability*

obtained. If the repeated experiment is then repeated a given number of times, say n, then n sets of observations are obtained. Each set of k observations is called a subgroup. Each subgroup has an average, a range, and a standard deviation. Consequently, three new data sets, consisting of second variables, are available. This concept is illustrated in Example 3.14.

Example 3.14

In an assembly process, an automatic device, called a probe station, measures the distance that 18 critical components are from a target dimension. The measurements are in mils and are interpreted as follows:

If measurement is	Dimension is
Negative	Smaller than target
Zero	Equal to target
Positive	Larger than target

Basic random experiment: A subassembly enters the probe station.

Outcome: The measurement obtained by Probe 16.

Repeat the experiment four times.

Repeat the repeated experiment 50 times. The results are shown in Table 3.4.

In this example 50 subgroups of size 4 are generated. The average, range, and standard deviation of each subgroup are provided in the table. Each may be considered as a second variable of the repeated random experiment. In what follows, each set of 50 observations of the second variable is discussed as a new set of data.

The reader should practice calculating the average, range, and standard deviation. Results can be verified by the table. The average and the standard deviation should be calculated for the three sets of data formed by the subgroup averages, the subgroup ranges, and the subgroup standard deviations. These also appear in the table.

Since this is the first example in which negative numbers appear, a few comments are in order.

1. If a set of numbers contains both positive and negative numbers, the maximum will be positive and the minimum will be negative. Consider subgroup 1.

    Outcomes: −0.065, 0.973, −0.136, 0.425

    Minimum = −0.136

    Maximum = 0.973

2. If a set of numbers contains only negative numbers, both the maximum and the minimum will be negative. Consider subgroup 11.

    Outcomes: −0.201, −0.114, −0.251, −0.234

    Minimum = −0.251

    Maximum = −0.114

Table 3.4 200 Measurements from Probe 16 in Subgroups of Size 4

Deviation from Target Dimension of Location 16 in Mils

Subgroup number	Measurements 1	2	3	4	Average	Range	Standard deviation
1	−0.06498	0.97281	−0.13580	0.42501	0.299260	1.10861	0.513625
2	0.11068	−0.02291	−0.10691	0.06101	0.010467	0.21759	0.095723
3	0.60827	−0.09569	0.26614	0.00192	0.195160	0.70396	0.314978
4	0.17987	−0.04712	0.00194	0.33270	0.116848	0.37982	0.173832
5	0.22028	0.29988	−0.10430	−0.02574	0.097530	0.40418	0.193170
6	0.27531	0.10603	0.08758	0.28930	0.189555	0.20172	0.107515
7	0.39073	−0.08042	−0.11251	0.03963	0.059357	0.50324	0.230415
8	−0.09392	−0.18294	0.14929	0.22340	0.023957	0.40634	0.193380
9	−0.13716	−0.12237	0.11997	−0.06200	−0.050390	0.25713	0.118135
10	−0.21634	−0.20332	0.21301	0.18230	−0.006088	0.42935	0.235655
11	−0.20065	−0.11430	−0.25137	−0.23396	−0.200070	0.13707	0.060929
12	0.01916	−0.22675	−0.26268	−0.33681	−0.201770	0.35597	0.154251
13	0.05439	0.24327	−0.14825	−0.09100	0.014602	0.39152	0.174685
14	0.21793	0.15421	0.27483	0.10529	0.188065	0.16954	0.073977
15	−0.20270	−0.14237	0.14738	0.10101	−0.024170	0.35008	0.174111
16	−0.01822	0.17071	0.31554	0.21162	0.169913	0.33376	0.139453
17	0.11995	−0.01525	0.14141	−0.06301	0.045775	0.20442	0.100343
18	−0.08117	0.14827	0.16517	−0.27718	−0.011228	0.44235	0.209903
19	0.05233	0.32564	−0.13274	−0.26620	−0.005243	0.59184	0.256354
20	−0.24138	0.28657	0.07182	0.31892	0.108983	0.56030	0.259035
21	0.16380	0.43774	−0.11506	−0.29143	0.048762	0.72917	0.319951
22	0.18507	0.03138	0.37611	0.06289	0.163863	0.34473	0.156254
23	−0.04116	0.38590	−0.15386	0.21059	0.100367	0.53976	0.243817
24	0.00019	−0.27440	0.09393	0.10719	−0.018273	0.38159	0.177269
25	−0.05649	−0.10793	−0.04274	−0.10956	−0.079180	0.06682	0.034604
26	0.08617	−0.27133	−0.21102	0.20358	−0.048150	0.47491	0.229308
27	−0.14026	0.01998	−0.22077	0.00042	−0.085158	0.24075	0.115187
28	0.23601	−0.19895	0.48261	0.33635	0.214005	0.68156	0.293333
29	0.38018	−0.18017	−0.06659	−0.07814	0.013820	0.56035	0.249516
30	−0.07728	−0.22895	−0.28519	−0.20149	−0.198228	0.20791	0.087836
31	−0.06632	0.15575	−0.15319	−0.17526	−0.059755	0.33101	0.151170
32	0.16338	0.03251	0.28541	0.24455	0.181462	0.25290	0.111503
33	−0.01891	−0.04474	−0.31447	0.16605	−0.053018	0.48052	0.197973
34	−0.07447	0.24251	0.45421	−0.23906	0.095798	0.69327	0.311504
35	0.74455	0.39230	−0.18358	−0.19471	0.189640	0.93926	0.460440
36	−0.00810	0.13172	0.02959	0.52108	0.168573	0.52918	0.242315
37	−0.24461	−0.10053	0.04334	−0.19416	−0.123990	0.28795	0.126521
38	−0.14537	−0.24684	−0.03924	0.25809	−0.043340	0.50493	0.218097
39	0.00319	−0.10076	0.19513	0.24702	0.086145	0.34778	0.162863
40	−0.29943	0.07273	0.29520	−0.17393	−0.026358	0.59463	0.264300
41	−0.16119	−0.14278	0.66078	0.01582	0.093158	0.82197	0.386668
42	0.53656	−0.22735	−0.33897	−0.12122	−0.037745	0.87553	0.393057
43	−0.01626	−0.14288	0.04139	0.13841	0.005165	0.28129	0.117534
44	−0.01293	−0.16212	−0.27410	0.02469	−0.106115	0.29879	0.138020
45	0.02053	0.49720	−0.25452	0.14053	0.100935	0.75172	0.311666
46	−0.22419	0.14679	−0.29980	−0.27101	−0.162053	0.44659	0.208239
47	−0.33133	0.17746	0.05734	−0.06991	−0.041610	0.50879	0.217961
48	0.27851	0.26403	−0.05370	−0.19322	0.073905	0.47173	0.234982
49	−0.09353	−0.22078	0.30547	0.13171	0.030717	0.52625	0.234078
50	0.51955	0.20313	−0.22425	−0.00012	0.124578	0.74380	0.315913

3. If the minimum is negative, then the range requires the subtraction of a negative number.

Subgroup 1: R = Maximum − Minimum

$$= 0.973 - (-0.136)$$

$$= 0.973 + 0.136 = 1.109$$

Subgroup 11: R = Maximum − Minimum

$$= -0.114 - (-0.251)$$

$$= -0.114 + 0.251 = 0.137$$

Note that subtracting a negative number is equivalent to changing the sign of the number (to a positive number) and adding the result. If the operations are performed on a calculator for a negative number, enter the number without a sign and then depress the (+/−) key. The negative number will then appear in the window.

The reader should practice using negative numbers and use the table to verify results. Subgroups 11, 25, and 30 contain only negative numbers. Subgroups 6, 14, 22, and 32 are the only subgroups with only positive numbers.

The histogram of the individual observations is given in Figure 3.11. Note that it is not really bell-shaped. It is shifted to the left of its average ($\bar{X} = 0.033$ and $s = 0.232$). The three intervals, ($\bar{X} - s$ to $\bar{X} + s$), ($\bar{X} - 2 \times s$ to $\bar{X} + 2 \times s$), and ($\bar{X} - 3 \times s$ to $\bar{X} + 3 \times s$), are shown in the figure. A comparison of the predicted versus the actual number of observations is

Interval		Predicted		Actual	
From	To	Number	Percent	Number	Percent
$\bar{X} - s = -0.199$	$\bar{X} + s = 0.265$	137	68.27	133	66.6
$\bar{X} - 2 \times s = -0.431$	$\bar{X} + 2 \times s = 0.497$	191	95.45	192	96.0
$\bar{X} - 3 \times s = -0.663$	$\bar{X} + 3 \times s = 0.729$	199	99.73	198	99.0

The histogram of the subgroup averages is shown in Figure 3.12. Note that it is more nearly bell-shaped. The average of the subgroup averages is denoted by $\bar{\bar{X}}$ (pronounced x-bar-bar). Note that $\bar{\bar{X}} = 0.033$ and is the same value as the average of all the data. This will always occur; the

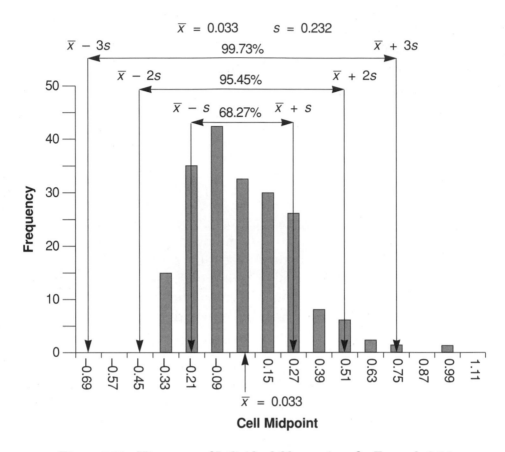

Figure 3.11   Histogram of Individual Observations for Example 3.14

average of the subgroup averages always is equal to the average of the individual observations. The standard deviation of the subgroup averages is denoted by $s_{\bar{x}}$. Here $s_{\bar{x}} = 0.116$. Note that $s_{\bar{x}} = s \div 2$. This is not accidental. If a subgroup size is k, the standard deviation of the subgroup averages will be approximately equal to the standard deviation of the individual observations divided by the square root of k. In symbols this is

$$s_{\bar{x}} = \frac{s}{\sqrt{k}}$$

For our example, $k = 4$, and

$$s_{\bar{x}} = \frac{s}{\sqrt{k}} = \frac{s}{\sqrt{4}} = s \div 2 = 0.232 \div 2 = 0.116.$$

The predicted distribution of the values of $\bar{X}$ (the subgroup averages) about their average ($\bar{\bar{X}}$) compared to the observed frequencies is

Interval		Predicted		Actual	
From	**To**	**Number**	**Percent**	**Number**	**Percent**
$\bar{\bar{X}} - s_{\bar{x}} = -0.083$	$\bar{\bar{X}} + s_{\bar{x}} = 0.149$	34	68.27	33	66.0
$\bar{\bar{X}} - 2 \times s_{\bar{x}} = -0.199$	$\bar{\bar{X}} + 2 \times s_{\bar{x}} = 0.265$	48	95.45	47	94.0
$\bar{\bar{X}} - 3 \times s_{\bar{x}} = -0.315$	$\bar{\bar{X}} + 3 \times s_{\bar{x}} = 0.381$	50	99.73	50	100

These intervals are shown in Figure 3.12.

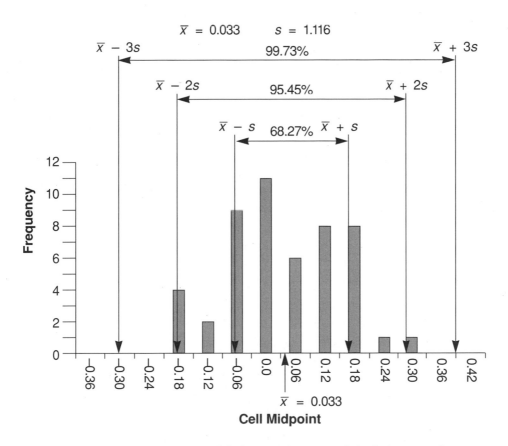

Figure 3.12   Histogram of Subgroup Averages of 50 Subgroups of Size 4 from Example 3.14

The fact that the histogram of the subgroup averages is approximately bell-shaped also is not accidental. In fact, as the subgroup size increases, the histogram of the subgroup averages becomes even closer to a bell-shaped histogram. Example 3.15 provides a more dramatic illustration of this concept.

Figures 3.13 and 3.14 show histograms of the subgroup ranges and standard deviations, respectively. Generally, the histograms of these two second variables will not be bell-shaped. The average and standard deviation of the subgroup ranges are denoted by $\bar{R}$ and s_R, respectively. The average and standard deviation of the subgroup standard deviations are denoted by $\bar{s}$ and s_S, respectively. Values of, $\bar{R}$, s_R, $\bar{s}$, and s_S for this example are

$$\bar{R} = 0.461 \qquad s_R = 0.219$$
$$\bar{s} = 0.209 \qquad s_S = 0.100$$

Both $\bar{R}$ and $\bar{s}$ can be used to estimate $s_{\bar{x}}$, and hence s. This estimation is covered in Chapter 4 and is used extensively in the construction of control charts.

The important observation for these second variables at this point is simply that new data sets were constructed from an existing data set. These new data sets have measures of both central tendency and variation. It also is of note that the variation in the subgroup averages always is less than the variation in the individual observations. Example 3.15 provides additional amplification of these concepts.

Example 3.15

An art gallery routinely evaluates objects on display. The evaluation consists of asking visitors to rank an object on a scale from 0 to 10. The ranks correspond to the degree that a visitor likes or dislikes an art object. A rank of 0 corresponds to abhorrence of the object, 5 corresponds to indifference to the object, and 10 corresponds to adoration of the object.

Basic random experiment: A visitor is requested to evaluate a particular abstract painting.

Outcome: The actual evaluation by the visitor.

Repeat the experiment for four visitors.

Repeat the repeated experiment 50 times. The results of these 200 evaluations in subgroups of size 4 are shown in Table 3.5. The subgroup averages, ranges, and standard deviations also are shown.

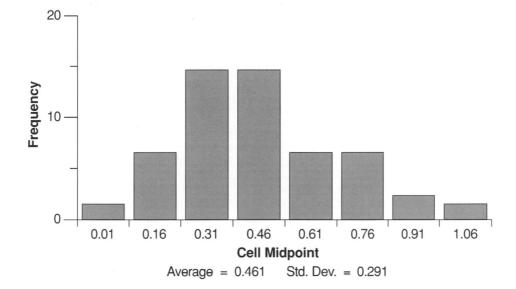

*Figure 3.13   Histogram of Subgroup Range for 50 Subgroups
of Size 4 from Example 3.14*

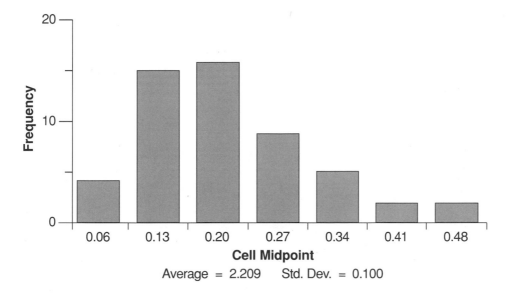

*Figure 3.14   Histogram of Subgroup Standard Deviations for
50 Subgroups of Size 4 from Example 3.14*

Table 3.5   200 Evaluations of an Abstract Painting in
Subgroups of Size 4

Subgroup number	Measurements (evaluations)				Average	Range	Standard deviation
	1	2	3	4			
1	7	3	5	1	4.00	6	2.58
2	5	1	6	1	3.25	5	2.63
3	6	0	4	7	4.25	7	3.10
4	10	1	2	2	3.75	9	4.19
5	10	0	7	6	5.75	10	4.19
6	10	6	8	8	8.00	4	1.63
7	7	10	2	1	5.00	9	4.24
8	2	10	6	9	6.75	8	3.59
9	3	8	9	6	6.50	6	2.65
10	6	4	8	1	4.75	7	2.99
11	0	6	5	4	3.75	6	2.63
12	7	9	3	2	5.25	7	3.30
13	8	2	6	4	5.00	6	2.58
14	4	1	2	3	2.50	3	1.29
15	0	9	10	7	6.50	10	4.51
16	10	7	5	1	5.75	9	3.77
17	1	7	10	2	5.00	9	4.24
18	5	7	3	4	4.75	4	1.71
19	1	2	1	0	1.00	2	0.82
20	5	7	2	4	4.50	5	2.08
21	10	2	2	7	5.25	8	3.95
22	9	7	3	1	5.00	8	3.65
23	5	4	10	0	4.75	10	4.11
24	0	9	2	1	3.00	9	4.08
25	10	4	2	9	6.25	8	3.86
26	10	8	6	8	8.00	4	1.63
27	6	6	9	5	6.50	4	1.73
28	6	7	1	3	4.25	6	2.75
29	2	6	8	3	4.75	6	2.75
30	5	1	10	1	4.25	9	4.27
31	4	0	6	0	2.50	6	3.00
32	9	2	8	2	5.25	7	3.77
33	2	2	3	1	2.00	2	0.82
34	10	1	3	9	5.75	9	4.43
35	1	5	0	3	2.25	5	2.22
36	9	8	4	9	7.50	5	2.38
37	10	7	7	6	7.50	4	1.73
38	4	2	8	5	4.75	6	2.50
39	9	6	7	5	6.75	4	1.71
40	0	5	7	4	4.00	7	2.94
41	3	2	10	3	4.50	8	3.70
42	2	9	9	5	6.25	7	3.40
43	9	2	6	9	6.50	7	3.32
44	5	2	10	5	5.50	8	3.32
45	4	8	5	10	6.75	6	2.75
46	7	9	5	1	5.50	8	3.42
47	0	1	8	10	4.75	10	4.99
48	0	7	5	0	3.00	7	3.56
49	2	3	9	6	5.00	7	3.16
50	7	7	5	3	5.50	4	1.91

The summary measures for the individual observations and the three subgroup second variables are

$$\bar{X} = 4.99 \qquad\qquad s = 3.16$$
$$\bar{\bar{X}} = 4.99 \qquad\qquad s_{\bar{X}} = 1.55$$
$$\bar{R} = 6.62 \qquad\qquad s_R = 2.11$$
$$\bar{s} = 3.01 \qquad\qquad s_s = 1.01$$

Note that $\bar{X} = \bar{\bar{X}}$ and that $s_{\bar{X}}$ is approximately one-half of s ($k = 4$ and $\sqrt{k} = \sqrt{4} = 2$).

The histograms for the individual observations and for the subgroup averages, ranges, and standard deviations are shown in Figures 3.15, 3.16, 3.17, and 3.18, respectively. The histogram of the individual observations is close to a rectangular box and is definitely not bell-shaped. The histogram of the subgroup averages, however, is approximately bell-shaped. This is a dramatic change. A comparison of the predicted frequencies versus the observed frequencies for both the individuals and the subgroup averages follows. Note that this prediction should not be made when the histogram is not approximately bell-shaped. In order to emphasize this point, however, the comparison for the individual observations is included for this example.

Predicted versus observed for individual observations

Interval		Predicted		Actual	
From	To	Number	Percent	Number	Percent
$\bar{X} - s = 1.83$	$\bar{X} + s = 8.15$	137	68.27	127	63.5
$\bar{X} - 2 \times s = -1.33$	$\bar{X} + 2 \times s = 11.31$	191	95.45	200	100
$\bar{X} - 3 \times s = -4.49$	$\bar{X} + 3 \times s = 14.47$	199	99.73	200	100

Predicted versus observed for subgroup averages

Interval		Predicted		Actual	
From	To	Number	Percent	Number	Percent
$\bar{\bar{X}} - s_{\bar{X}} = 3.44$	$\bar{\bar{X}} + s_{\bar{X}} = 6.54$	34	68.27	31	62.0
$\bar{\bar{X}} - 2 \times s_{\bar{X}} = 1.89$	$\bar{\bar{X}} + 2 \times s_{\bar{X}} = 8.09$	48	95.45	49	98.0
$\bar{\bar{X}} - 3 \times s_{\bar{X}} = 0.34$	$\bar{\bar{X}} + 3 \times s_{\bar{X}} = 9.64$	50	99.73	50	100

Many additional examples could be provided to illustrate this dramatic change in the shape of the histogram of the individual observations to that of the subgroup averages. Figures 3.19 and 3.20 suffice to illustrate

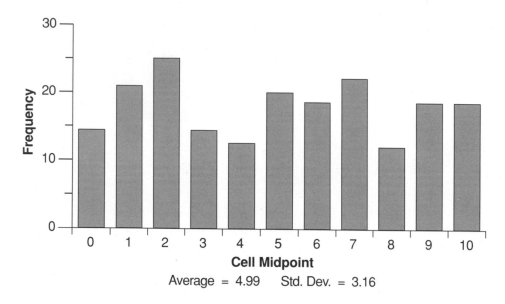

Figure 3.15   Histogram of 200 Evaluations of an Abstract Painting

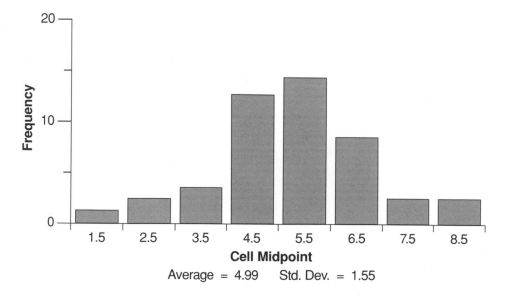

Figure 3.16   Histogram of Subgroup Averages of 200 Evaluations
of an Abstract Painting with a Subgroup Size of 4

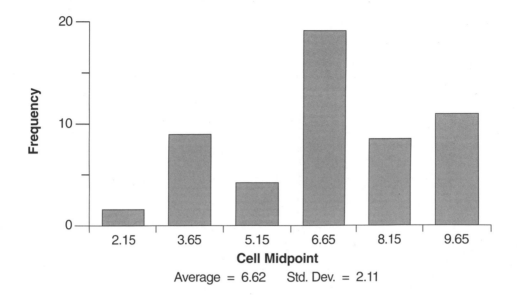

Figure 3.17   Histogram of Subgroup Ranges for 200 Evaluations of an Abstract Painting with a Subgroup Size of 4

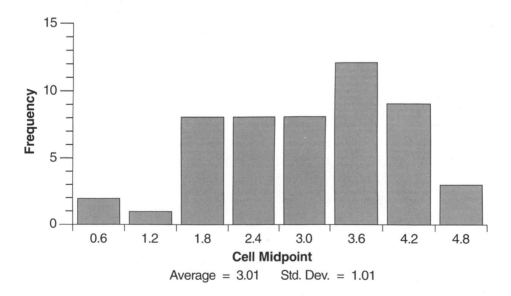

Figure 3.18   Histogram of Subgroup Standard Deviations of 200 Evaluations of an Abstract Painting with a Subgroup Size of 4

this phenomenon graphically. The histograms in Figure 3.19 change from a triangle to a bell. The change in Figure 3.20 is to a bell from a smooth curve starting at a positive height for a value of an observation of 0 and decreasing in size as the value of the observation decreases.

The histograms of the subgroup ranges and standard deviations (see Figures 3.17 and 3.18) again are not bell-shaped.

Summary

The important concepts in this chapter were

1. In order to understand a system, it is necessary to think like a statistician.

2. Thinking like a statistician involves

   a. transforming common, everyday events into basic random experiments.

   b. defining an outcome of interest.

   c. collecting data by repeating the basic random experiment.

3. The system will exhibit variation; the data collected will have variation.

4. Summary measures are convenient devices to describe the central tendency of the data (average) and the variation in the data (range or standard deviation).

5. Histograms are graphical displays of data sets. They illustrate both the central tendency and the inherent variation of the data.

6. The bell-shaped histogram is important. It permits one to predict the number of observations that will be contained in specified intervals.

7. Subgroups are formed by repeating a repeated random experiment. The second variables of these subgroups form new data sets. These new data sets are useful in later work.

8. Regardless of the shape of the histogram of the individual observations, the histogram of the subgroup averages will be approximately bell-shaped. This forms the basis of an important concept in statistical control charts. This concept will be used and amplified in the following chapters.

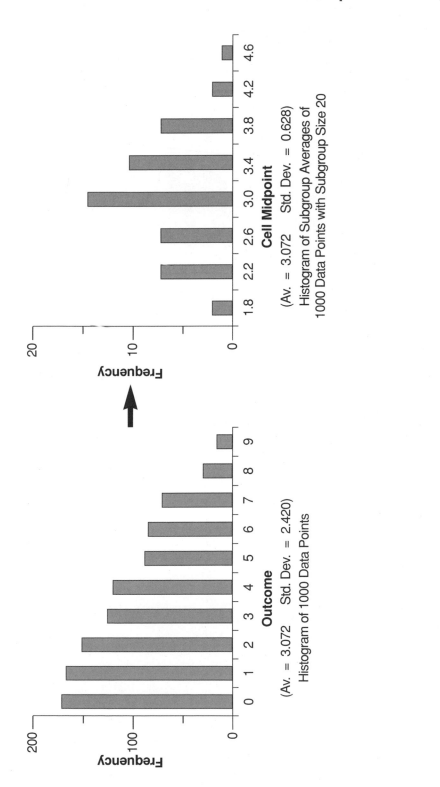

Figure 3.19 Illustration of Change in Histogram Shape from Individual Observations to Subgroup Averages

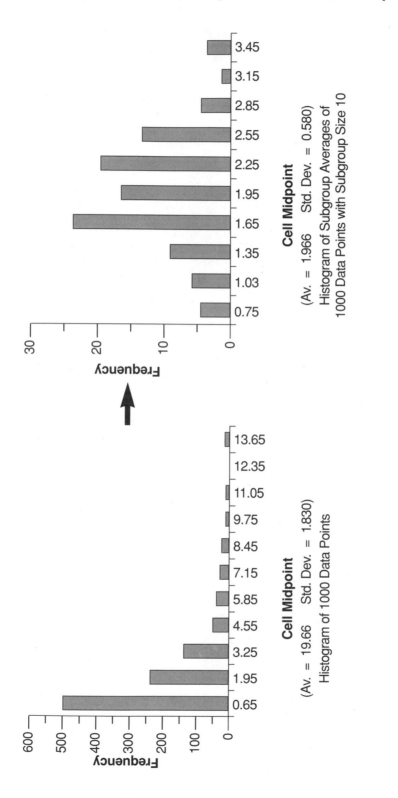

Figure 3.20   Illustration of Change in Histogram Shape from Individual Observations to Subgroup Averages

Select Bibliography

Bethea, R. M., Duran, B. S., and Boullion, T. L. *Statistical Methods for Engineers and Scientists*. New York: Marcel Dekker, 1975.

Bowker, A. H. and Lieberman, G. J. *Engineering Statistics*. 2nd ed. Englewood Cliffs, NJ: Prentice-Hall, 1972.

Devore, J. L. *Probability and Statistics for Engineering and the Sciences*. 2d ed. Monterey, CA: Brooks/Cole Publishing Company, 1987.

Guttman, I., Wilks, S. S., and Hunter, J. S. *Introductory Engineering Statistics*. 3d ed. New York: Wiley, 1982.

Koopmans, L. H. *An Introduction to Contemporary Statistics*. Boston: Duxbury Press, 1981.

Kvanli, A. H. *Statistics: A Computer Integrated Approach*. St. Paul, MN: West Publishing Company, 1988.

Lapin, L. L. *Probability and Statistics for Modern Engineering*. Boston: PWS Publishers, 1983.

McClure, J. T. and Dietrich, F. H. *Statistics*. 3d ed. San Francisco: Dellen Publishing Co., 1985.

Mendenhall, W., Scheaffer, R. L., and Wackerly, D. D. *Mathematical Statistics with Applications*. 4th ed. Boston: Duxbury Press, 1990.

Miller, I. and Freund, J. F. *Probability and Statistics for Engineers*. 2d ed. Englewood Cliffs, NJ: Prentice-Hall, 1977.

Ott, L. *An Introduction to Statistical Methods and Data Analysis*. Boston: Duxbury Press, 1977.

Papoulis, A. *Probability and Statistics*. Englewood Cliffs, NJ: Prentice-Hall, 1990.

Ross, S. *A First Course in Probability*. 2d ed. New York: MacMillan, 1989.

Scheaffer, R. L. and McClure, J. T. *Probability and Statistics for Engineers*. Boston: Duxbury Press, 1986.

Wheeler, D. J., and Chambers, D. S. *Understanding Statistical Process Control*. Statistics Process Controls Inc., 1986.

Chapter 4
Construction and Use of Control Charts

Introduction

In the Deming philosophy of management the new way of conducting business is management by involvement (MBI). In this type of management it is assumed that 80 to 95 percent of all problems are with the system and that everyone must understand the system. In order to understand the system it is essential to understand variability. Since statistics is the study of variability, it is essential to understand statistics. Statistical control charts are important in the general subject of statistical process control (SPC). These charts are mathematical techniques to help us understand and control the variability that is exhibited by a process.

For any process it is possible to identify two general categories of variability into which all causes of variability can be placed. The first general category is called *natural variability*. The second is called *assignable* (or unnatural) *variability*. Anyone who is familiar with a process that exhibits variability usually can identify a large number of factors that contribute, in an unexplainable way, to the variability of the process. These factors are referred to as natural causes of variability. For example, temperature, atmospheric pressure, humidity, worker differences, vibration, and other environmental factors all may be natural causes of variability. No one really can identify how these factors actually affect variability. We only know that they have an impact on variability. In an everyday situation think of the gas mileage between fill-ups of a car. There are many causes of natural variability (for example, weather, traffic, and so on).

Any cause of variability that cannot be identified as natural is referred to as an assignable cause and is categorized as unnatural variability. Some people call these special causes. Examples of unnatural causes of variability are tool wear, machine wear, voltage or power surges, bad materials, or an untrained worker. In the example on gas mileage, a fouled spark plug may represent an assignable cause of variability. Generally, when a process is operating with only natural causes of variability, it is possible to observe the process at points in time and, with a basic understanding of statistics, answer the question:

> Is it very likely that the process is continuing to
> operate with only natural variability?

This is exactly the situation encountered when one begins to apply the general techniques of statistics and, in particular, when a statistical control chart is used.

In the use of the statistical control chart, the amount of variability exhibited by the numbers is examined and a decision is made about the process from which the numbers were drawn. It must be decided if the process is operating with only natural variability (a *state of statistical control*) or if the process is operating with unnatural variability. If the numbers indicate that unnatural variability is present, then a search begins for the assignable cause(s) that produced the unnatural variability. If not, the process will be left alone and allowed to operate with only natural variability. In this decision-making process the objective is to return the system to a state of natural variability. The decision-making process is continued by collecting more data and by repeating analysis of the facts.

A statistical control chart is a technique for providing a graphical display of the numbers to assist in making a correct decision about the state of statistical control of the process. The chart simply is a plot of the value of a second variable that is computed from a series of repetitions (a subgroup) of a basic random experiment. The chart, along with basic rules about the behavior of the chart for a process which is in statistical control, will provide the proper structure to reach a logical conclusion.

In the construction of a control chart, the repeated experiments are called subgroups, and one value of the second variable of interest is plotted for each subgroup. Thus, the vertical axis of the control chart is the second variable and the horizontal axis is the subgroup number (or 1, 2, 3, 4, . . . , r; where r is the number of subgroups observed to date).

The chart also will have three horizontal lines called the upper control limit (UCL), the lower control limit (LCL), and the center line (CL). The general format of the statistical control chart is shown in Figure 4.1.

The central tendency and the standard deviation of the second variable are used to determine values for the CL, the UCL, and the LCL. In general, the CL is the central tendency of the second variable, the UCL is the central tendency plus three standard deviations of the second variable, and the LCL is the central tendency minus three standard deviations. For all types of control charts and for a process that is in statistical control, the central tendency and the standard deviation of the second variable can be related to the central tendency and the standard deviation of the basic experiment. In this manner, and using some additional knowledge of probability theory and statistics, the following statement can be made:

> If the process is in a state of statistical control, then the second variable should behave in a random but natural way. If your plotted values of the second variable do not behave as they should, then the only conclusion is that the process is not operating in a state of statistical control.

The basic elements of statistics were presented in Chapter 3. Both the concept of a histogram and certain summary measures of a set of data that were called the average (central tendency) and the standard deviation (dispersion) were introduced. The bell-shaped histogram and its important characteristics also were introduced. This introduction to statistics is sufficient to understand the basics of the statistical control chart.

The Process of Control Charting

In the construction and use of any type of statistical control chart a three-phase procedure is followed. In the first phase the natural variability of the process must be defined. This phase involves the repetitive process shown in Figure 4.2 and generally is referred to as "construction of trial control charts." It is important to emphasize that the initial set of data should consist of at least 25 subgroups. Furthermore, if subgroups are eliminated due to the identification and removal of assignable causes, additional data must be collected to have at least 25 subgroups in the data set used to recompute the CL, the UCL, and the LCL. It also is important to point out that data should not be discarded unless an assignable cause is identified and eliminated from the process. Attempts to bring an

What Does a Statistical Control Chart Look Like?

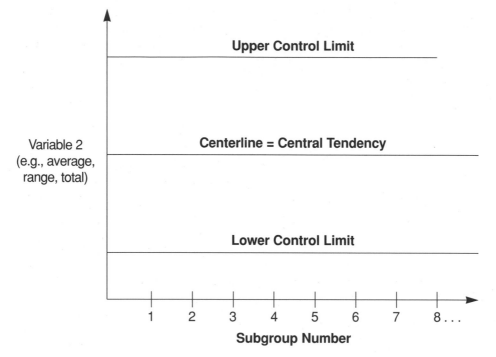

Figure 4.1   General Format of a Statistical Control Chart

out-of-control process into statistical control by identifying and removing sources of *unnatural* variation usually require a significant amount of time and energy.

After the control chart has been constructed and the values of the important second variable have been plotted, one must decide if the process is operating with only natural variability *(statistical control)* or with unnatural variability *(out of statistical control)*.

If any of the following conditions exist, it is generally accepted that one should search for the cause or causes of unnatural variability.

1. A value of the second variable is plotted above the UCL or below the LCL.

2. Eight consecutive values of the second variable appear above the CL or below the CL.

3. Twelve out of 14 consecutive values of the second variable are either above the CL or below the CL.

Trial Control Charting

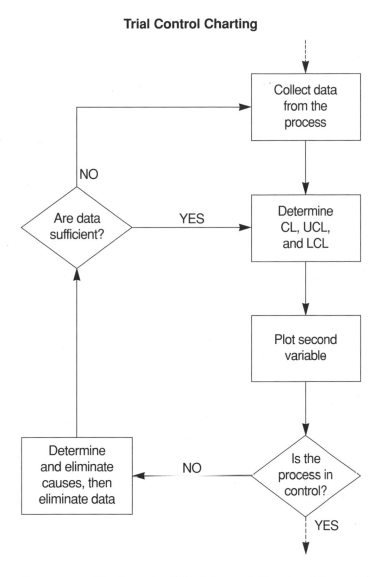

Figure 4.2   The Process of Trial Control Charting (Phase 1)

4. Six consecutive values of the second variable show either an increasing trend or a decreasing trend.

5. The values of the second variable demonstrate cyclical or periodic behavior.

It should be emphasized that these rules generally are acceptable in the use of statistical control charts. When a specific situation is studied, a careful analysis should be made of the cost of making incorrect decisions. In order to accomplish this task you must determine the cost of saying that the process is in control when it is not. Similarly you must determine the cost of saying the process is not in control when it is. Once these costs have been established, the rules outlined herein and the corresponding risks can be evaluated. In many cases the rules might have to be adjusted to reflect the costs.

Once the natural variability of the process is established then the second phase can be initiated. In this phase one begins to monitor the process and to use the control chart as illustrated by the flow chart shown in Figure 4.3. When monitoring the process, the emphasis is on identifying and removing sources of *unnatural* variation, which occur when one or more assignable causes force an in-control process to go out of statistical control.

The third phase of control charting focuses on improving the process and is illustrated in Figure 4.4. In attempting to improve the process, considerable effort is spent identifying and removing sources of *natural* variation. When the process has been improved or significantly changed

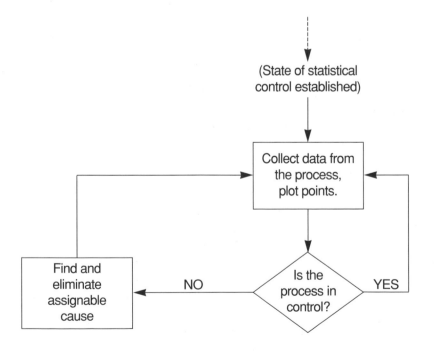

Figure 4.3   Monitoring the Process to Maintain Control (Phase 2)

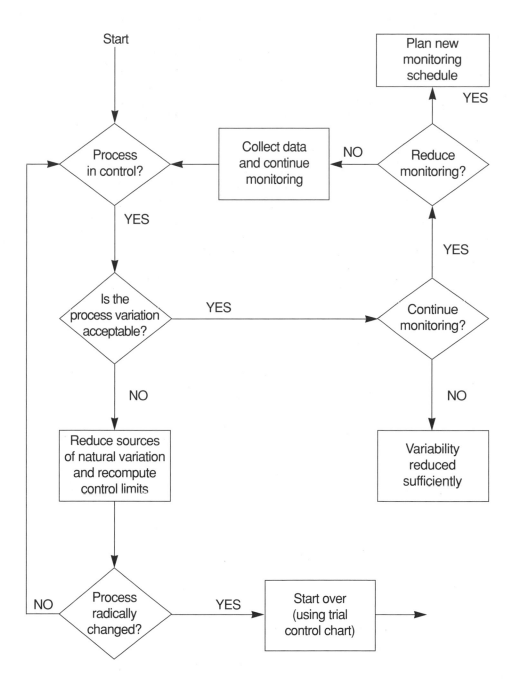

Figure 4.4   Improving the Process (Phase 3)

in any way, the control limits and the center line of the control chart should be recomputed. Reducing the natural variability of the process will narrow the distance between the UCL and LCL.

Chapter 5 discusses the subject of process capability. Once this topic is understood, the statistical control chart is used as a valuable tool in helping to decide if the process should be monitored less frequently or if monitoring should be discontinued altogether. Reduced and discontinued monitoring are desirable. They indicate that the variability of the process is reduced to an acceptable level and that the process is in, and probably will remain in, a state of statistical control. The behavior and capability of the process probably will continue to be acceptable. Ideally the objective of SPC is to reach a point where the process is operating in a natural state of variability without the need for SPC. Namely, the ideal objective of SPC is to put yourself, as a statistician, out of business.

Specific Types of Statistical Control Charts

Most practical decision-making situations that should be analyzed with the help of a statistical control chart can be placed into one of three categories. These are referred to in this chapter as Categories I, II, and III. A description of each category and the important second variables that are commonly used in each category follows.

Category I: Repeated experiments (the subgroup) where the outcome of each trial is

0 (conforming) or 1 (nonconforming).

Important Second Variable: Fraction nonconforming in the subgroup.

Category II: Repeated experiments (the subgroup) where the outcome of each trial is

0 or 1 or 2 or 3 or . . . (for example, nonconformities).

Important Second Variable: Total number of nonconformities in the subgroup.

Category III: Repeated experiments (the subgroup) where the outcome of each trial is

Measurable (continuous).

Important Second Variables: subgroup average, subgroup range, subgroup standard deviation.

Now that the general procedure for constructing and using statistical control charts has been described, it remains to discuss the specifics of each type of control chart. Each of the aforementioned charts will be discussed.

Category I–The Discrete Random Experiment: Fraction Nonconforming Chart

In this case it is assumed that data have been collected for r subgroups where each of the k items in a subgroup has been classified as either non-conforming or conforming. The number of nonconforming items for each subgroup is then presented in tabular form as shown in Table 4.1.

Table 4.1   Number of Nonconforming Items in Each Subgroup

Subgroup number	Number of nonconforming items in subgroup
1	n_1
2	n_2
3	n_3
:	:
:	:
:	:
$r-1$	$n_r - 1$
r	n_r

Using the values shown in Table 4.1, the average value of the fraction nonconforming is then computed as follows:

$$\bar{p} = \text{Average value of fraction nonconforming} = \frac{n_1 + n_2 + \ldots + n_r}{k \times r}$$

The center line and the control limits are then computed to be

$$\text{Center line (CL)} = \bar{p},$$

$$\text{Upper control limit (UCL)} = \bar{p} + \frac{3}{\sqrt{k}} \sqrt{\bar{p}(1 - \bar{p})}, \text{ and}$$

$$\text{Lower control limit (LCL)} = \bar{p} - \frac{3}{\sqrt{k}} \sqrt{\bar{p}(1 - \bar{p})}.$$

For ease of computation the value of $\dfrac{3}{\sqrt{k}}$ for different values of k is given in Table 4.2. If the LCL is computed to be a negative value, it should be set equal to zero.

Once the control chart has been constructed, the fraction nonconforming for each subgroup is plotted on the control chart and an assessment of the state of statistical control is made. As an example of a fraction nonconforming control chart, consider a situation where electrical switches are classified as either nonconforming or conforming and that 30 subgroups, each consisting of 40 switches, were examined, with the resulting number of nonconforming items shown in Table 4.3. In this situation $\bar{p} = 0.079$, $k = 40$, and from Table 4.2, $3 \div \sqrt{k} = 0.4743$. The control limits are then computed as follows:

Table 4.2   Value of $3 \div \sqrt{k}$ versus k

Subgroup size (k)	Factor $3 \div \sqrt{k}$	Subgroup size (k)	Factor $3 \div \sqrt{k}$	Subgroup size (k)	Factor $3 \div \sqrt{k}$
2	2.1213	22	0.6396	42	0.4629
3	1.7321	23	0.6255	43	0.4575
4	1.5000	24	0.6124	44	0.4523
5	1.3416	25	0.6000	45	0.4472
6	1.2247	26	0.5883	46	0.4423
7	1.1339	27	0.5774	47	0.4376
8	1.0607	28	0.5669	48	0.4330
9	1.0000	29	0.5571	49	0.4286
10	0.9487	30	0.5477	50	0.4243
11	0.9045	31	0.5388	51	0.4201
12	0.8660	32	0.5303	52	0.4160
13	0.8321	33	0.5222	53	0.4121
14	0.8018	34	0.5145	54	0.4082
15	0.7746	35	0.5071	55	0.4045
16	0.7500	36	0.5000	56	0.4009
17	0.7276	37	0.4932	57	0.3974
18	0.7071	38	0.4867	58	0.3939
19	0.6882	39	0.4804	59	0.3906
20	0.6708	40	0.4743	60	0.3873
21	0.6547	41	0.4685	61	0.3841

Table 4.3 Number of Nonconforming Items in 40 Electrical Switches

Subgroup number	Number of nonconforming items
1	3
2	3
3	2
4	7
5	1
6	3
7	3
8	3
9	2
10	5
11	7
12	1
13	2
14	4
15	3
16	4
17	4
18	8
19	2
20	3
21	2
22	2
23	4
24	2
25	4
26	3
27	2
28	2
29	2
30	2

$$\text{CL} = \bar{p} = 0.079$$

$$\text{UCL} = \bar{p} + \frac{3}{\sqrt{k}} \sqrt{\bar{p}\,(1 - \bar{p})} = 0.207$$

$$\text{LCL} = \bar{p} - \frac{3}{\sqrt{k}} \sqrt{\bar{p}\,(1 - \bar{p})} = -0.049.$$

Since the computed value for LCL is negative, LCL = 0. The fraction nonconforming can *never* be less than zero.

The control chart and a plot of the fraction nonconforming for each subgroup is shown in Figure 4.5. Since the process appears to be in a state of statistical control, the control chart would be used for monitoring the process.

Category II–The Discrete Random Experiment: Total Number of Nonconformities

In this case it is assumed that data have been collected for r subgroups where, in each subgroup, there are k items. Each item will have 0, 1, 2, 3, . . . nonconformities and the total number of nonconformities for the subgroup is reported as shown in Table 4.4. Using the values in Table 4.4, the average value of the total number of nonconformities is then computed as follows:

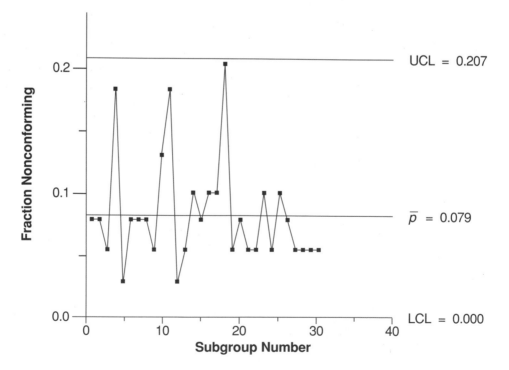

Figure 4.5   Control Chart for Fraction Nonconforming Light Switches

Table 4.4 Number of Nonconformities in Each Subgroup

Subgroup number	Number of nonconforming items in subgroup
1	T_1
2	T_2
3	T_3
$\vdots$	$\vdots$
$r-1$	$T_r - 1$
r	T_r

$\overline{T}$ = Average value of total number of nonconformities

$$= \frac{T_1 + T_2 + \ldots + T_r}{r}.$$

The center line and the control limits are then computed to be:

$$\text{Center line (CL)} = \overline{T},$$

$$\text{Upper control limit (UCL)} = \overline{T} + 3\sqrt{\overline{T}}, \text{ and}$$

$$\text{Lower control limit (UCL)} = \overline{T} - 3\sqrt{\overline{T}}.$$

If LCL is computed to be a negative value it is set equal to zero. Again, the total number of nonconformities for each subgroup would be plotted on the control chart to determine if the process is in a state of statistical control.

In most texts on statistical process control, this control chart is called a c-chart. Here the symbol "T" is used to refer to "total," instead of the standard use of the symbol c.

As an example of this type of control chart, consider a situation in which each subgroup consists of 30 plates of steel and the total number of nonconformities for the 30 plates was counted for each of 50 subgroups. The results are shown in Table 4.5.

In this situation $\overline{T}$ = 13.86 and the center line and control limits are computed as follows:

Table 4.5   Total Number of Nonconformities in 30 Plates of Steel

Subgroup number	Total number of nonconformities	Subgroup number	Total number of nonconformities
1	15	26	18
2	13	27	13
3	12	28	15
4	15	29	14
5	7	30	12
6	18	31	14
7	8	32	6
8	15	33	8
9	11	34	18
10	16	35	10
11	18	36	24
12	12	37	10
13	11	38	12
14	15	39	20
15	16	40	13
16	16	41	12
17	13	42	13
18	17	43	17
19	13	44	17
20	12	45	13
21	12	46	19
22	12	47	18
23	17	48	13
24	12	49	12
25	12	50	14

$$\text{Center line (CL)} = \overline{T} = 13.86,$$

$$\text{Upper control limit (UCL)} = \overline{T} + 3\sqrt{\overline{T}} = 25.03,$$

$$\text{Lower control limit (UCL)} = \overline{T} - 3\sqrt{\overline{T}} = 2.69.$$

The total number of nonconformities for each subgroup is plotted on the control chart in Figure 4.6. Again, the control chart indicates a state of statistical control.

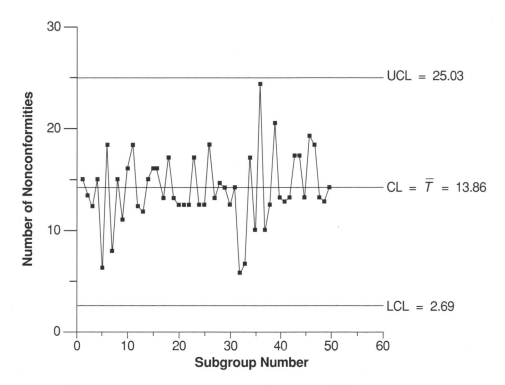

Figure 4.6   Control Chart for Total Number of Nonconformities

Category III–The Continuous Random Experiment ($\bar{X}$ *Chart*, **R** *Chart*)

In this case it is assumed that data have been collected from the process and that k measurements of the continuous variable of interest have been made for each of r subgroups. For each subgroup the average value ($\bar{X}$) and the range (R) have been calculated and conveniently displayed as shown in Table 4.6.

Using the notation given in Table 4.6, the following computations are made:

$$\bar{\bar{X}} = \text{the average of the subgroup averages}$$

$$= \frac{\bar{X}_1 + \bar{X}_2 + \ldots + \bar{X}_r}{r}, \text{ and}$$

$$\bar{R} = \text{the average of the subgroup ranges}$$

$$= \frac{\bar{R}_1 + \bar{R}_2 + \ldots + \bar{R}_r}{r}.$$

Table 4.6 Subgroup Data from Process (Average and Range)

Subgroup number	Measurements for subgroup				Average subgroup ($\bar{X}$)	Range of subgroup (R)
1	X_{11}	X_{12}	X_{13}	$\ldots X_{1k}$	$\bar{X}_1$	R_1
2	X_{21}	X_{22}	X_{23}	$\ldots X_{2k}$	$\bar{X}_2$	R_2
3	X_{31}	X_{32}	X_{33}	$\ldots X_{3k}$	$\bar{X}_3$	R_3
$\vdots$					$\vdots$	$\vdots$
$r-1$	$X_{(r-1)1}$	$X_{(r-1)2}$	$X_{(r-1)3}$	$\ldots X_{(r-1)k}$	$\bar{X}_{r-1}$	R_{r-1}
r		X_{r1}	X_{r2}	$X_{r3} \ldots X_{rk}$	$\bar{X}_r$	R_1

These two values are then used to determine the center line and the control limits for the $\bar{X}$ and R charts as follows:

$\bar{X}$ Chart

$$\text{Center line (CL)} = \bar{\bar{X}},$$
$$\text{Upper control limit (UCL)} = \bar{\bar{X}} + A_2\bar{R}, \text{ and}$$
$$\text{Lower control limit (LCL)} = \bar{\bar{X}} - A_2\bar{R}.$$

The value of A_2 can be determined from Table 4.7.

R Chart

$$\text{Center line (CL)} = \bar{R},$$
$$\text{Upper control limit (UCL)} = D_4\bar{R}, \text{ and}$$
$$\text{Lower control limit (LCL)} = D_3\bar{R}.$$

The value of D_3 and D_4 are also determined from Table 4.7.

As an example of the use of $\bar{X}$ and R charts, consider the situation where a laborer is using a shovel to move material from a pile into a hopper. Before each full shovel is placed into the hopper it is weighed, with the results shown in Table 4.8. For this situation the control charts for the average and range would be established as follows:

Average

$$\text{Center line (CL)} = \bar{\bar{X}} = 49.75,$$
$$\text{Upper control limit (UCL)} = \bar{\bar{X}} + A_2\bar{R} = 63.38, \text{ and}$$
$$\text{Lower control limit (LCL)} = \bar{\bar{X}} - A_2\bar{R} = 36.13.$$

Table 4.7   Factors for $\bar{X}$ and R Charts

Subgroup Size	Value of factor		
(*k*)	A_2	D_4	D_3
2	1.880	3.267	0
3	1.023	2.574	0
4	0.729	2.282	0
5	0.577	2.115	0
6	0.483	2.004	0
7	0.419	1.924	0.076
8	0.373	1.864	0.136
9	0.337	1.816	0.184
10	0.308	1.777	0.223

Table 4.8   Measured Values of a Quality Characteristic with Subgroup Average, Range, and Standard Deviation

Subgroup number	Measurements					Average	Range	Standard deviation
	1	2	3	4	5			
1	58.950	51.480	64.510	52.930	42.330	54.040	22.180	8.346
2	67.110	46.830	58.030	38.030	56.800	53.360	29.080	11.184
3	70.150	43.830	73.370	48.080	50.240	57.134	29.540	13.597
4	50.570	45.990	49.500	39.150	51.200	47.282	12.050	4.972
5	60.910	46.140	58.720	47.520	46.180	51.894	14.770	7.293
6	34.000	45.880	49.550	42.830	40.420	42.536	15.550	5.870
7	55.860	51.930	49.990	52.860	33.740	48.876	22.120	8.722
8	52.700	68.690	67.690	41.790	32.870	52.748	35.820	15.753
9	44.580	34.920	45.270	43.320	48.060	43.230	13.140	4.959
10	41.220	54.600	52.560	59.310	40.590	49.656	18.720	8.358
11	56.110	60.970	69.270	53.020	36.220	55.118	33.050	12.217
12	56.570	33.800	60.660	43.530	47.370	48.386	26.860	10.665
13	45.660	49.170	52.860	62.080	78.160	57.586	32.500	13.028
14	30.600	49.070	57.650	62.050	48.080	49.490	31.450	12.076
15	44.150	79.840	51.750	37.490	53.050	53.256	42.350	16.128
16	65.420	50.810	42.990	39.780	27.080	45.216	38.340	14.168
17	40.780	52.490	37.850	51.080	36.610	43.762	15.880	7.495
18	49.950	40.630	41.590	48.470	47.150	45.558	9.320	4.193
19	38.160	56.080	43.710	58.910	59.230	51.218	21.070	9.668
20	37.680	40.180	64.660	43.640	61.800	49.592	26.980	12.669
21	40.670	42.370	62.520	52.710	46.510	48.956	21.850	8.889
22	55.630	35.070	49.090	52.820	55.640	49.650	20.570	8.582
23	50.750	47.930	56.720	48.140	57.770	52.262	9.840	4.697
24	56.950	38.030	49.720	49.710	51.030	49.088	18.920	6.867
25	58.130	29.920	46.440	42.320	43.030	43.968	28.210	10.095

Range

$$\text{Center line (CL)} = \bar{R} = 23.61,$$

$$\text{Upper control limit (UCL)} = D_4\bar{R} = 49.93, \text{ and}$$

$$\text{Lower control limit (LCL)} = D_3\bar{R} = 0.000.$$

The resulting $\bar{X}$ and R charts and the plotted values for each subgroup are shown in Figure 4.7. Again, it would be determined that the process is in a state of statistical control.

If the process is out of control in this decision-making process, the objective is to return the system to its state of natural variability and to continue the decision-making process by collecting more data (the facts) and by repeating your analysis of the facts.

Category III–The Continuous Random Experiment ($\bar{X}$ Chart, S Chart)

This case is similar to the previous one in that it is assumed that data have been collected from the process and that k measurements of the continuous variable of interest have been made for each of r subgroups. For each subgroup the average value ($\bar{X}$) and the standard deviation have been calculated and are conveniently displayed as shown in Table 4.9.

Using the notation given in Table 4.9, the following computations are made:

$$\bar{\bar{X}} = \text{the average of the subgroup averages}$$

$$= \frac{\bar{X}_1 + \bar{X}_2 + \ldots + \bar{X}_r}{r}, \text{ and}$$

Table 4.9 Subgroup Data from Process
(Average and Standard Deviation)

Subgroup number	Measurements for subgroup				Average of subgroup ($\bar{X}$)	Std. dev. of subgroup (S)
1	X_{11}	X_{12}	X_{13}	$\ldots \; X_{1k}$	$\bar{X}_1$	S_1
2	X_{21}	X_{22}	X_{23}	$\ldots \; X_{2k}$	$\bar{X}_2$	S_2
3	X_{31}	X_{32}	X_{33}	$\ldots \; X_{3k}$	$\bar{X}_3$	S_3
$\vdots$					$\vdots$	$\vdots$
$r-1$	$X_{(r-1)1}$	$X_{(r-1)2}$	$X_{(r-1)3}$	$\ldots \; X_{(r-1)k}$	$\bar{X}_{r-1}$	S_{r-1}
r	X_{r1}	X_{r2}	X_{r3}	$\ldots \; X_{rk}$	$\bar{X}_r$	S_1

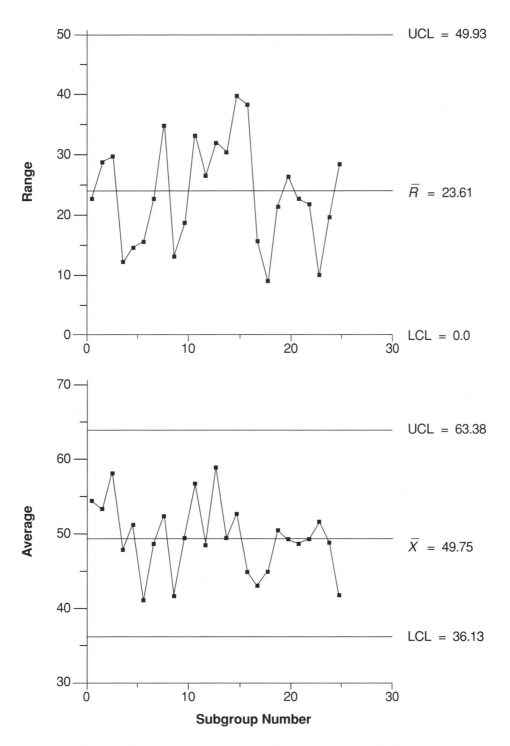

Figure 4.7   Average and Range Charts for Data in Table 4.8

$$\bar{S} = \text{the average of the subgroup ranges}$$

$$= \frac{S_1 + S_2 + \ldots + S_r}{r}.$$

These two values are then used to determine the center line and the control limits for the $\bar{X}$ and S charts as follows:

$\bar{X}$ Chart

Center line (CL) = $\bar{\bar{X}}$,

Upper control limit (UCL) = $\bar{\bar{X}} + A_3\bar{S}$, and

Lower control limit (LCL) = $\bar{\bar{X}} - A_3\bar{S}$.

The value of A_3 can be determined from Table 4.10.

S Chart

Center line (CL) = $\bar{S}$,

Upper control limit (UCL) = $B_4\bar{S}$, and

Lower control limit (LCL) = $B_3\bar{S}$.

The value of B_3 and B_4 are also determined from Table 4.10.

As an example of the use of $\bar{X}$ and S charts consider the data shown in Table 4.8. If the column for the range is ignored then the format is as shown in Table 4.9. For this situation the control chart for the average weight would be established as follows:

$\bar{X}$ Chart

Center line (CL) = $\bar{\bar{X}}$ = 49.75,

Upper control limit (UCL) = $\bar{\bar{X}} + A_3\bar{S}$ = 63.48, and

Lower control limit (LCL) = $\bar{\bar{X}} - A_3\bar{S}$ = 36.03.

S Chart

Center line (CL) = $\bar{S}$ = 9.62,

Upper control limit (UCL) = $B_4\bar{S}$ = 20.10, and

Lower control limit (LCL) = $B_3\bar{S}$ = 0.00.

The resulting $\bar{X}$ and S charts and the plotted values for each subgroup are shown in Figure 4.8. Again, it would be concluded that the process is in a state of statistical control.

Because the range is easier to compute than the standard deviation, historically $\bar{X}$ and R charts were used more frequently than $\bar{X}$ and S charts.

Table 4.10 Factors for $\bar{X}$ and S Charts

Subgroup size	Value of factor		
(k)	A_3	B_3	B_4
2	2.659	0	3.267
3	1.954	0	2.568
4	1.628	0	2.266
5	1.427	0	2.089
6	1.287	0.030	1.970
7	1.182	0.118	1.882
8	1.099	0.185	1.815
9	1.032	0.239	1.761
10	0.975	0.284	1.716
11	0.927	0.321	1.679
12	0.886	0.354	1.646
13	0.850	0.382	1.618
14	0.817	0.406	1.594
15	0.789	0.428	1.572
16	0.763	0.448	1.552
17	0.739	0.466	1.534
18	0.718	0.482	1.518
19	0.698	0.497	1.503
20	0.680	0.510	1.490
21	0.663	0.523	1.477
22	0.647	0.534	1.466
23	0.633	0.545	1.455
24	0.619	0.555	1.445
25	0.606	0.565	1.435

With the availability of statistical calculators and personal computers the use of $\bar{X}$ and S charts will increase. Also, the reader should be warned that the $\bar{X}$ and R charts should not be used when the number of observations in the subgroup is large (greater than about 10). In these cases the $\bar{X}$ and S charts should be used.

Summary of Statistical Control Charts

In this chapter two control charts for discrete control charts were developed. For continuous random experiments, a set of two control

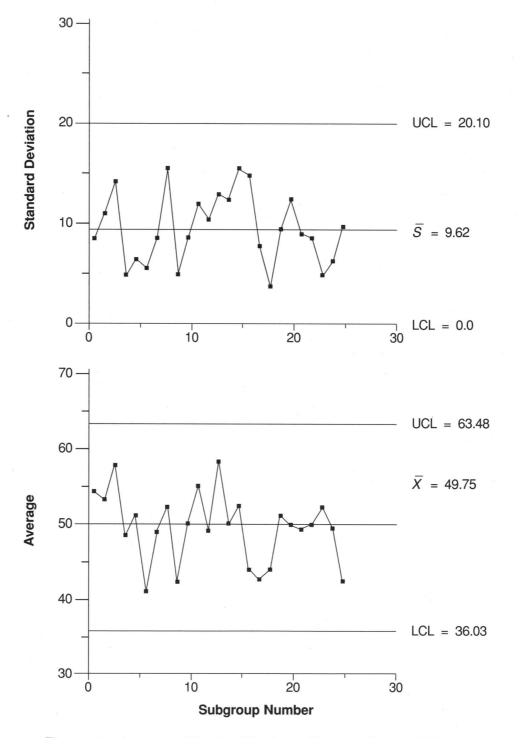

Figure 4.8   Average and Standard Deviation Charts for Data in Table 4.8

charts, called X-bar ($\bar{X}$) and R charts, were developed for the situation in which the range was used to measure variability. When the standard deviation is used to measure variability, a different set of control charts (X-bar and S charts) were employed.

Select Bibliography

Automotive Industry Action Group and the Automotive Division of ASQC. *Fundamental Statistical Process Control Reference Manual.* Milwaukee, WI: ASQC Quality Press, 1992.

Banks, J. *Principles of Quality Control.* New York: Wiley, 1981.

Duncan, A. J. *Quality Control and Industrial Statistics.* 5th ed. Homewood, IL: Irwin, 1986.

Doty, L. A. *Statistical Process Control.* Milwaukee, WI: ASQC Quality Press, 1991.

Fellers, G. *SPC for Practitioners: Special Cases and Continuous Processes.* Milwaukee, WI: ASQC Quality Press, 1991.

Gitlow, H. S. "Product Defects and Productivity," *Harvard Business Review*, Vol. 61, No. 5: 131–141 (Sept./Oct. 1983).

Grant, E. L. and Levenworth, R. S. *Statistical Quality Control.* 5th ed. New York: McGraw-Hill Book Co., 1980.

Keats, J. B. and Montgomery, D. C. *Statistical Process Control in Manufacturing.* Milwaukee, WI: ASQC Quality Press, 1991.

Mauch, P. D. *Basic SPC: A Guide for the Service Industries.* Milwaukee, WI: ASQC Quality Press, 1991.

Montgomery, D. C. *Introduction to Statistical Quality Control.* New York: Wiley, 1985.

Shewhart, W. A. *The Economic Control of Quality of Manufactured Product.* New York: D. Van Nostand & Co., 1980 (originally published in 1931).

———. *Statistical Method from the Viewpoint of Quality Control.* New York: Dover Publications, 1986 (originally published in 1939).

Chapter 5
Process Capability Analysis

Introduction

If a system has a measurable quality characteristic that has been determined to be in a state of statistical control then, and only then, can the ability of the system to meet engineering specifications be examined. This is called *process capability analysis*. Usually at this point at least 25 subgroups of measurements on the quality characteristic have been obtained. The average $\bar{X}$ and the standard deviation s of the individual measurements should be calculated and a histogram of the individual measurements should be constructed. If the histogram is approximately bell-shaped, then a standard process capability analysis can be done.

In the subsequent sections three cases are considered. First it is assumed that the measured quality characteristic has a lower specification limit (LSL), an upper specification limit (USL), and a target value (T). In the second case the quality characteristic has only a USL; no target value (T) is specified. In the third case the quality characteristic has only a lower specification limit (LSL). Again, no target value is specified.

Case 1: USL, LSL, and T

In this case the engineering specifications should be checked to determine if the target value is located correctly. If the histogram of the quality characteristic is approximately bell-shaped, then the best target value should be midway between the upper specification limit and the lower specification limit. Therefore, T should equal (USL + LSL) ÷ 2. The reason for this becomes clear upon examination of the histograms shown in Figure 5.1. In Figure 5.1(a) the histogram of the quality characteristic is shown to be centered on T = (USL + LSL) ÷ 2 or midway between the specification limits. The nonconforming product includes those measurements above USL and below LSL. If the histogram is not centered on T and is shifted away from T, as shown in Figure 5.1(b), then an increase in nonconforming product results. A shift in the opposite direction is shown in Figure 5.1(c). Again an increase in nonconforming product is the result. It can be shown mathematically that, for a quality characteristic with a histogram that is symmetric about the average, the location of the target value that minimizes nonconforming product is midway between USL and LSL or at $T = (USL + LSL) \div 2$.

If, in conducting a process capability analysis, one finds that engineering has specified a target value that is not the best, then the situation should be examined thoroughly to determine the reason.

The next step in a process capability analysis is to make a computation called the *process capability index* (PCI) where PCI = (USL – LSL) $\div$ (6s). The numerator of this expression (USL – LSL) is called the tolerance range TR and s is the standard deviation of the quality characteristic. In the traditional approach to process capability analysis, the computed value of the PCI is used to obtain an indication of the ability of the process to meet engineering specifications. For example, in a book by Montgomery[1] minimum values for PCI are recommended. The PCI should be approximately 1.33 for an existing process and 1.50 for a new process. The PCI by itself, however, is not a meaningful number. The PCI must be examined simultaneously with the process average $\overline{X}$ and its relationship to the target value T. The importance of this statement is illustrated for an extreme case in Figure 5.2. From the values given in Figure 5.2, the PCI is computed to be 1.33. Note, however, that the process is producing 100 percent nonconforming product.

As as alternative to the PCI, C_{pk} is a measure of process capability that penalizes the system for being away from the best target value. C_{pk} is the smaller of the following two values:

$$\frac{USL - \overline{X}}{3s} \quad \text{or} \quad \frac{\overline{X} - LSL}{3s}$$

If $\overline{X}$ is at the optimal target value of $(USL + LSL) \div 2$, then $C_{pk} = PCI$.

In addition to understanding the meaning of the PCI and the C_{pk} it is also important to understand the relationship between these indices and the fraction of nonconforming product. If the process average $\overline{X}$ is on the optimal target value $T = (USL + LSL) \div 2$, Table 5.1 shows the relationship between the PCI and the number of nonconforming parts per million (NCPPM) produced.

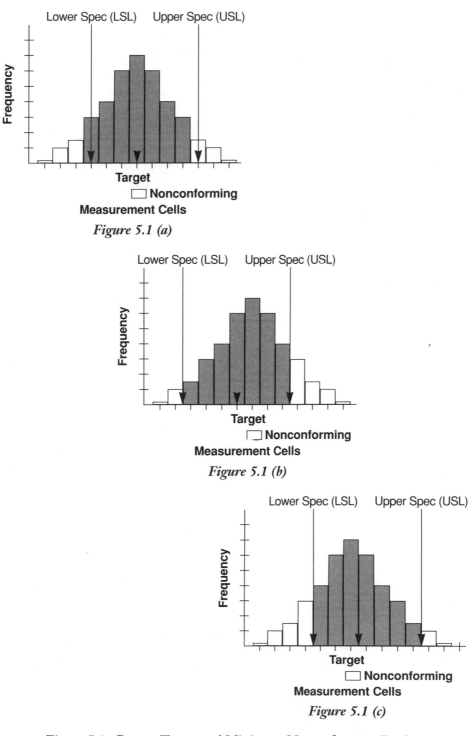

Figure 5.1 (a)

Figure 5.1 (b)

Figure 5.1 (c)

Figure 5.1   Process Target and Minimum Nonconforming Product

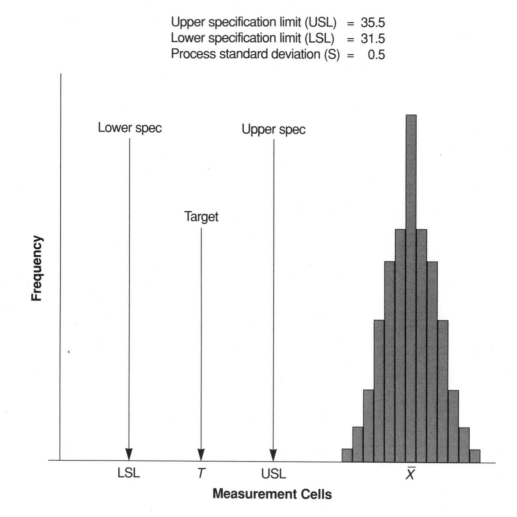

Upper specification limit (USL) = 35.5
Lower specification limit (LSL) = 31.5
Process standard deviation (S) =   0.5

Figure 5.2   Extreme Case: Acceptable PCI, Poor Performance

The values presented in Table 5.1 are important in understanding the relationship between the PCI and NCPPM, but only when a histogram of the data is bell-shaped. It could be argued that the actual objective in a process capability analysis is to determine the rate at which nonconforming items are produced, and NCPPM is therefore a more meaningful expression of process capability. The PCI and the C_{pk} have no direct physical meaning and therefore are artificial indices.

Once the process capability analysis has been conducted, the situation can be examined to determine if the system needs improvement and,

Table 5.1   Process Capability Index and Nonconforming Parts per Million—Given the Average Measurement $\overline{X}$ Is Located at the Optimal Target $T = (USL + LSL) \div 2$

PCI	Nonconforming parts per million
0.50	133,624
0.75	24,456
1.00	2,700
1.10	967
1.20	318
1.30	96
1.40	27
1.50	7
1.60	2
1.70	0
1.80	0
2.00	0

if so, to determine the type of improvement that can be made. In this analysis one should consider first the relationship between $\overline{X}$ and T. If $\overline{X}$ is not approximately equal to T, then an immediate improvement can be made to the process by making an adjustment (if possible) to center the process on T. If the system still needs improvement, then the only solution is to change the process to decrease the standard deviation s to obtain a more acceptable value for the PCI or the C_{pk}.

Example 5.1

An automobile manufacturer is concerned about the front-end alignment of the cars produced in a plant. One of the measurements of front-end alignment is camber, the angle in degrees of the front wheel from a vertical plane as viewed from the front of the car. A perfectly vertical wheel has zero camber. If the wheel is not perfectly vertical and if the top of the wheel is closer to the centerline of the car, the camber angle is said to be negative. If the top of the wheel is farther from the centerline of the car, the camber angle is said to be positive.

A run of 98 cars was used to determine the process capability of the machine that is used to set camber. The histogram was bell-shaped with $\overline{X} = 0.0000$ and $s = 0.1468$ and control charts indicated that the system was in a state of statistical control.

The engineering department has provided the following specifications for camber measurements:

USL: +0.5 (degrees)

Target Value: 0.0 (degrees)

LSL: −0.5 (degrees)

To calculate the PCI, the tolerance range TR must be computed. Remember that the $TR = \text{USL} - \text{LSL}$ and therefore, $TR = 0.5 - (-0.5) = 1.0$. The PCI is then computed to be:

$$PCI = TR \div (6 \times s), \text{ or}$$

$$PCI = 1.0 \div ((6)(0.1468)) = 1.14.$$

From Table 5.1, the number of nonconforming parts per million for this process is between 318 and 967.

If the process were not centered at the optimal target value (for example, suppose $\bar{X} = 0.1775$) then the C_{pk} would be the smaller of the two values:

$$\frac{(0.5000 - 0.1775)}{3\,(0.1468)} = 0.732 \text{ or } \frac{(0.1775 - (-0.5000))}{3\,(0.1468)} = 1.539$$

Therefore $C_{pk} = 0.732$. Note that the C_{pk} is lower than the PCI.

Once the process is centered on the target value, the number of nonconforming parts can be reduced only by reducing the variability, or the standard deviation, of the process. That reduction might be achieved by better operator training, better machine maintenance, improved control of incoming parts and material, or by using more capable equipment.

Case 2: One-Sided Process Capability— USL Only

In this case it is assumed that the quality characteristic has been determined to be in a state of statistical control with a histogram that is approximately bell-shaped with an average $\bar{X}$ and a standard deviation s. Engineering has specified the upper specification limit (USL) for the quality characteristic. No target value T is specified. Since no target value is specified, the process should be operated with the lowest $\bar{X}$ that is realistic. This statement becomes clear upon examination of the two histograms shown in Figure 5.3. A decrease in the process average increases the quality of the process.

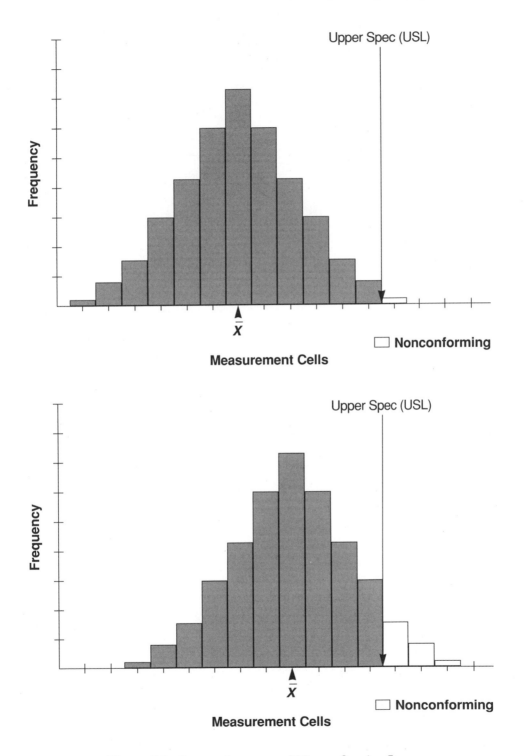

Figure 5.3   Process Average and Nonconforming Items

In this case the process capability index, PCI, is defined to be:

$$PCI = (USL - \bar{X}) \div 3s.$$

As seen in the two-sided case, recommended minimum values have been suggested.[1] The PCI should be at least 1.25 for an existing process and 1.45 for a new process. The number of nonconforming parts per million is directly related to the PCI and is shown in Table 5.2.

Table 5.2   One-Sided Process Capability Index and
Nonconforming Parts Per Million

PCI	Nonconforming parts per million
0.50	66,800
0.75	12,200
1.00	1,350
1.10	483
1.20	159
1.30	48
1.40	13
1.50	3.4
1.60	0.8
1.70	0.2
1.80	0.03
2.00	0

Case 3: One-Sided Process Capability— LSL Only

In the case where engineering has specified only a lower specification limit (LSL), the quality of the process is increased as the process average $\bar{X}$ is increased. This fact is illustrated by the histograms shown in Figure 5.4. In this case the process capability index PCI is given by

$$PCI = (\bar{X} - LSL) \div 3s.$$

The recommended minimum values for the PCI and the relationship between the PCI and the number of nonconforming parts per million are the same as the previous case. Again, the relationship between the PCI and NCPPM is shown in Table 5.2.

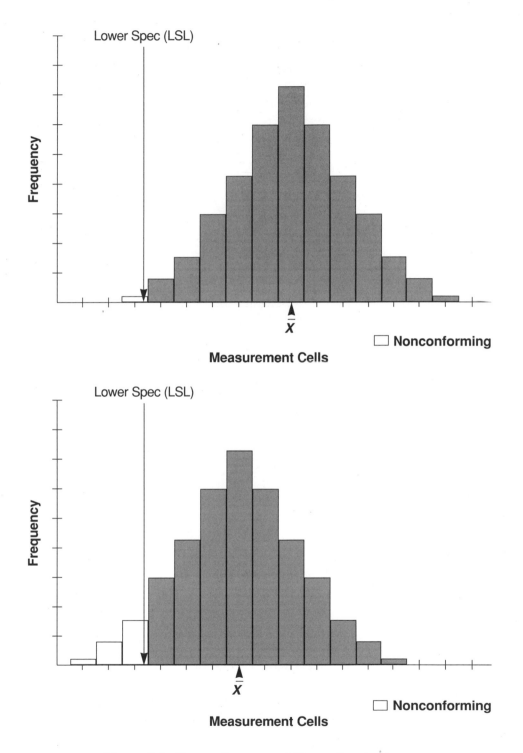

Figure 5.4   Process Average and Nonconforming Items

Process Capability Indices as Second Variables

Remembering that a second variable is a number computed from the outcomes of repeated basic random experiments (see p. 26), the process capability indices are second variables. This means that PCI and C_{pk} should be thought of in exactly the same fashion as the average and standard deviation. Averages and standard deviations computed from a number of samples exhibit variability, and have histograms with a characteristic shape. Exactly the same situation would apply if process capability indices are computed repeatedly, even if the process *remained in statistical control.*

It is very important to understand the behavior of the histograms of process capability indices. In this section, the behavior of C_{pk} is illustrated using the following example:

> A process has been operating in a state of statistical control for a long time, and a histogram of the quality characteristic measurements has a bell shape. The average of the measurements is 87.5, and the standard deviation is 15.625. The engineering department has imposed a USL of 150, and a LSL of 25. It can be verified that the process is operating at the best target value to minimize nonconforming product, and that the C_{pk} of these measurements is 1.333.

Now consider a random experiment. Forty parts are produced by the process, and the measurements from those parts are used to compute an average, a standard deviation, and a C_{pk} value. Each of these is a second variable, and we would expect each to vary somewhat from the "true," or long-term values, given above.

This experiment was repeated 500 times, and in each repetition we used a computer to "produce" 40 parts. For each repetition of the experiment, the 40 measurements were used to compute the average, the standard deviation, and C_{pk}. Histograms of these second variables are shown in Figure 5.5.

The histogram of C_{pk} values can be used to estimate the chance of exceeding a particular value of C_{pk} when this type of experiment is performed. These results are shown in Table 5.3. Remember that the true value of C_{pk} for this process is 1.333. The chance of getting a C_{pk} value of 1.333 or above is only about 36 percent. In other words, there is a

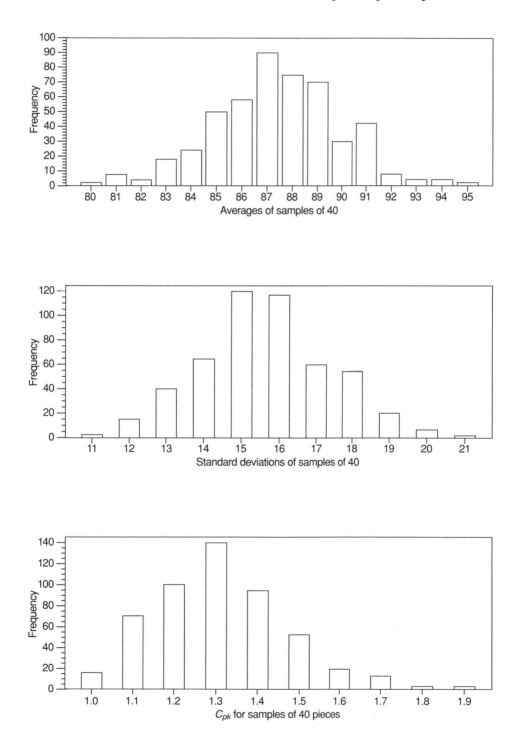

Figure 5.5   Histograms of Second Variables

64 percent chance of getting a value of C_{pk} that is less than the true value for this situation.

This is an extremely important result. If a customer demands that a supplier's process must operate with a C_{pk} value of 1.333, and further that this must be demonstrated in a 40-piece experiment, then even if the true C_{pk} of the process is 1.333 the customer is forcing the supplier to gamble on the process with loaded dice. Unfortunately, such demands are too common and they neglect the fundamental principle of process capability analysis. Process capability analysis is intended to be a long-term measure of the ability of a process to meet specifications. A single experiment of 40 pieces, 100 pieces, or even 500 pieces is not sufficient to judge the long-term performance of most processes.

Table 5.3   Chances of Exceeding C_{pk} Values
Based on 500 Repetitions of a 40-Piece Experiment

C_{pk} (midpoint)	Frequency	Chance of exceeding (percent)
1.0	14	97.20
1.1	67	83.80
1.2	100	63.80
1.3	138	36.20
1.4	93	17.60
1.5	56	6.40
1.6	20	2.40
1.7	9	0.60
1.8	2	0.20
1.9	1	0.00

Reference

1. Montgomery, D. C. *Introduction to Statistical Quality Control.* New York: Wiley, 1985.

Select Bibliography

Banks, J. *Principles of Quality Control.* New York: Wiley, 1981.

Burke, R. J., Davis, R. D., and Kaminsky, F. C. "Responding to Statistical Terrorism in Quality Control," *Transactions of the 47th Annual Quality Control Conference of the Rochester Section of ASQC* (March 12, 1991).

Chan, L. K., Cheng, S. W., and Spiring, F. A. "A New Measure of Process Capability: C_{pm}," *Journal of Quality Technology*, Vol. 20, No. 3 (July 1988).

Davis, R. D. and Kaminsky, F. C. "Statistical Measures of Process Capability and Their Relationship to Nonconforming Product," *Proceedings of the National Machine Tool Builders Association* (October 1989).

Dovich, R. A. "Statistical Terrorists," *Quality in Manufacturing Magazine* (March–April, 1991).

Duncan, A. J. "Process Capability Studies," *Proceedings, Middle Atlantic Conference*, American Society for Quality Control (February 1958).

————. *Quality Control and Industrial Statistics.* 5th ed. Homewood, IL: Irwin, 1986.

Gunter, B. "The Use and Abuse of C_{pk}," 4 parts, *Quality Progress* (January 1989, March 1989, May 1989, and July 1989).

Juran, J. M. *Juran's Quality Control Handbook.* New York: McGraw-Hill, 1988.

Kane, V. E. "Process Capability Indices," *Journal of Quality Technology*, Vol. 18, No. 1, pp. 41–52 (January 1986).

Chapter 6
Putting It All Together

In this book the reader was introduced to the Deming philosophy of management and to several problem-solving skills that can be used in the workplace to assist in the tremendous task of continuous improvement. Creating an environment to implement these techniques in the workplace is not an easy task. Problem-solving skills and statistical process control are not magic and their use does not provide a guarantee of quality. Without a true commitment to quality from upper levels of management, applications of problem-solving techniques and statistical process control are doomed to failure. In the words of Dr. Deming:

> He that starts with statistical methods alone will not
> be here in three years.

There is no single, correct approach that will guarantee the successful implementation of statistical process control. There is, however, a consensus among quality professionals on the need to satisfy certain prerequisites in the process of changing the organization's culture. The quality pyramid that was discussed in Chapter 1, and was presented in Figure 1.1, is intended to emphasize the point that a philosophical commitment to quality is essential. The commitment to quality must be established at the highest levels of the organization. Every upper level executive should be trained in the topics covered in this book. They must practice management by involvement (MBI), and they should become involved with cross-functional teams that apply these techniques to problems in the workplace.

When upper-level management realize that they must change their way of doing business the implementation of statistical process control can begin. This is how it might happen:

Hardy Case, General Manager of the Spheroids Division of the Northampton Round Widget Corporation, knew that there was a problem. The marketing manager's presentation made it clear that their share of the market was shrinking, and the production manager's estimate made it clear that production cost also was going to increase. He wanted to get to the bottom of this. When he asked why sales were dropping, the marketing manager's reply was concise: "The competition sells better stuff for less." The production manager could not explain why the competition's costs were lower. They bought their materials from some of the same suppliers and had the same labor contracts. It was a mystery.

At the next staff meeting, Case and his managers debated the issue. Some thought that robotics would be the answer, but someone pointed out that the competition did not use robots. Besides, the company had no money to invest. A magazine article about improving quality to reduce costs was passed around the table. No one could understand how costs could go down as quality went up. The article mentioned a seminar on the subject, and lacking a better idea, Case decided to go to the seminar.

Case was excited when he came back from the seminar. He was convinced that the new approach might just work for them, but the others were not easily persuaded. Case suggested that an in-house seminar should be arranged for the management. A consultant was retained, and a day-long seminar was arranged. When it was over, most of the staff agreed that improving quality might be the solution to both decreasing market share and increasing cost.

The upper management team must be trained in all of the topics covered in this book. During the training this team would select an area that needs improvement in the organization. Applying the problem-solving techniques, the team would construct a process flow diagram, use brainstorming, fishbone diagrams, and Pareto analysis to identify areas where statistics and statistical process control should be implemented to get control of the process.

> The consultant who presented the one-day seminar had made it clear that eventually *everyone* in the business would need training in problem solving and statistical techniques. The production manager said that she would not feel comfortable if these techniques were used in the plant before she learned them. Case saw the wisdom in this and suggested that the division management staff be trained first.
>
> The training was very time demanding. The managers were not accustomed to being away from their jobs so much, but the consultant insisted that the weekly training sessions were too important to be interrupted. The managers learned the techniques of brainstorming, process flow diagramming, basic statistics, and Pareto analysis. As an exercise they decided to apply these techniques to their own quality problems, using data from the finance and production departments. They were surprised to learn that 70 percent of their quality problems occurred in the expander and polishing processes.

As the management team becomes directly involved in the process, they will need the help and knowledge of those who work directly with the process. The need for training in the workforce will be revealed, and an organization-wide strategy for training can be developed.

> As the training sessions for the top managers continued, they could not forget the results of the exercise. When they learned about fishbone diagrams, they decided they should apply them to the expander and finishing processes to determine where SPC might be effective. They soon realized that none of them knew enough about the processes, so they invited the supervisors from those areas to join them. They explained what they were trying to do, but the supervisors did not volunteer much information, and they appeared quite uncomfortable. The group adjourned for a week.

Later, the finishing supervisor told the production manager that he and the other supervisors did not understand what all this statistics stuff was about. The manager quickly tried to explain about natural variability and statistical control, but she did not seem to get anywhere. An hour later she walked into Case's office and said, "I think we are going to have to train the supervisors too." Case heard her out and agreed. They talked to the two supervisors, who agreed to do it, but they thought that some of the production workers should be trained or they probably would not cooperate. Case and the production manager decided that a limited number of volunteers from the production line should be included.

Most organizations do not have qualified trainers. They must be hired or, alternatively, an outside consultant must be engaged. Quick "Train the Trainer" programs usually will not satisfy a company's needs. Trainers must be actively and enthusiastically involved in the application of problem-solving techniques and statistical process control, but they need to be knowledgeable about the use of these techniques. In addition, this knowledge and enthusiasm must be communicated in a classroom setting.

The finance manager did not want to use the consultant's services to do the additional training. He said it was too expensive, and that one of the mangers should do it instead. The consultant remarked that statistics could be very dangerous in unskilled hands, and pointed out the fact that managers all had full-time jobs to do besides the training. The production manager suggested that the consultant should start the new training program while helping the division to find a qualified, statistically trained person to hire. The finance manager grumbled, but Case liked the idea.

Training should be conducted over an extended period of time in sessions of four to six hours each. This allows the employees an opportunity to absorb the material and to apply the concepts between sessions.

A meeting was set up between the division management staff and the consultant to plan the training for the supervisors. The consultant reminded them that eventually everyone in the division would need training, and he recommended that they plan to give everyone exactly the same training. The marketing manager argued that production workers did not need the same level of understanding, and the finance manager pointed out the production quotas would be missed if too many workers were pulled off the line for an extended period of time.

The consultant was ready for them. He pointed out that if SPC was perceived as an "Us-and-Them" program, the workforce would never buy into it, and that the workers might need every bit as much understanding as the managers or supervisors because they were the ones minding the processes. He also said that training should not be done more quickly than SPC could be implemented, as implied by Deming's PDCA cycle. He suggested that the training schedule should be restricted to a fairly modest amount of time every week. Production would not suffer if a small amount of overtime was authorized.

Trainees should be encouraged to apply the problem-solving techniques as part of their job. At this point the management commitment to quality will become evident. Positive results achieved from such on-the-job applications should be presented to future training sessions. As with any other process, the training process should be improved by using the Deming Plan-Do-Check-Act cycle.

The training for the managers was completed, and the sessions for the supervisors and workers from the expander and polishing processes were in full swing. Rumors were flying around the plant floor, and the workers who had volunteered were catching some flak in the cafeteria. Some people thought that the volunteers were being "brainwashed."

The production manager told Case that she was going to drop in at that day's training session, and asked him to come along. They arrived to find the participants doing a fishbone diagram of the pitting problem in the polishing process. Case restrained himself from joining in the discussion, but when it was over, one of the workers challenged him. "When are we going to start keeping control charts on grit diameter?" he was asked. Case answered "As soon as you know how to do it. Let me know when you are ready. I want to see the first trial control chart."

Rumors flew around the cafeteria again the next morning. Why was Case going to look at a control chart? Some said it was a new way of keeping tabs on the workers. Some said it meant layoffs. Some were just curious about this SPC thing. Why was Case so interested in it?

Case did go down to see the first trial control chart, and over the course of two weeks he saw several more charts, because the process was not in control. Eventually the worker identified several assignable causes, and with the help of the supervisor and the production manager, they were eliminated. When the control chart indicated that the process was stable, Case asked the worker to carry out a process capability study, and to present the results to the next training session. The entire division management staff was there to hear the presentation.

As more teams are formed, they become involved in the collection and analysis of data. The types of data that are routinely collected by the organization, and how these data are related to problem solving and decision making, will change significantly as the need grows for data that are meaningful to continuous improvement.

The rumors were thicker than ever, but the supervisors were being flooded with volunteers for the next group to be trained. As the expander and polishing processes improved, groups were chosen from other processes, including purchasing and finance.

Things have been looking up a bit. Production costs have been coming in below estimate, and market share has gone up a little. The production manager and the finance manager have been going over the budget proposal for next year. The finance manager has no quarrel with the amount budgeted for training, but the production manager is not happy with the financial data available to her. "I want to make a statistical analysis of production costs before the new product is released to manufacturing," she said, "but these finance reports use a cost center breakdown that doesn't fit the process flow diagram."

The finance manager agreed that the reports would not help, so they were discontinued. The new approach turned out to require much less paperwork.

It should be understood clearly that the commitment to quality will not happen overnight. It will take a long time and it will require the expenditure of resources, particularly employees' time allocated to training. When upper-level management understands the concept of natural variability and, by their actions, demonstrate that they are not managing by tampering, the groundwork has been laid for process improvement. Understanding variability, training, and applying statistics to control the process are not process improvement. Process improvement only begins when these steps are complete.

Things are different at Spheroids. When Case was promoted to corporate vice president, the production manager was assigned his job. The division quality coordinator reports to her, and the people in the old QC department are now working on special projects instead of doing inspections. The consultant who helped the division with its first steps in SPC has finally retired and gone fishing.

There are all sorts of new approaches being taken. The engineering department now works with production and purchasing when they design a new product. Experimentation is going on in the lab to make sure that both the production and in-service performance of the new products are statistically stable under a variety of conditions. People who used to

> talk about baseball now discuss statistics, but rumors still fly around the cafeteria.

The fable is somewhat real. We have encountered most of these reactions, although not all in the same business.

This book ends as it started.

> Improve quality, you automatically improve productivity. You capture the market with lower price and higher quality. You stay in business, and you provide jobs. So simple.

> –W. E. Deming

Index